Alphabet PUPPETS

Editorial Development: Joy Evans
De Gibbs
Copy Editing: Cathy Harber
Laurie Westrich
Art Direction: Cheryl Puckett
Cover Design: David Price
Illustration: Shirley Beckes
Design/Production: Yuki Meyer

Congratulations on your purchase of some of the finest teaching materials in the world.

For information about other Evan-Moor products, call 1-800-777-4362, fax 1-800-777-4332, or visit our Web site, www.evan-moor.com.

18 Lower Ragsdale Drive, Monterey, CA 93940-5746. Printed in China.

Correlated to State Standards Visit *teaching-standards.com* to view a correlation of this book's activities to your state's standards. This is a free service.

Contents

Teaching with Alphabet Puppets

Make *Alphabet Puppets* a permanent addition to your classroom.

- Use them for lessons.
- Display them on bulletin boards.
- Put them in centers.
- Keep them available to students for playtime activities.

Puppets

Colorful animal characters visually stimulate student interest and alphabetic awareness.

Animal names introduce beginning sounds for each letter of the alphabet. The puppets for the letters ***a***, ***e***, ***i***, ***o***, and ***u*** introduce short vowel sounds and have special companion cards for the corresponding long vowel sounds. *(See "Long-Vowel Friends" on pages 218–224.)*

(front)

Bb
Ben, the bear
I am Ben, the bear.
Let's play a game.
Listen to the /b/ sound in my name.
Aa Bb Cc Dd Ee Ff Gg
Hh Ii Jj Kk Ll Mm Nn
Ss Tt Uu

(back)

Letter formation practice kinesthetically reinforces letter recognition. Numbered directional arrows guide the correct formation of each letter. *(A letter formation chart for the full alphabet is provided on page 217.)*

Rhyming chant provides verbal and auditory reinforcement of letter-sound relationships.

Alphabet chart illustrates the relative placement of letters and sounds.

Convenient pocket stores and displays picture cards.

Take-Home Mini-Puppets

So that students can have their own personal copies of the "animal alphabet" to take home, each unit includes a reproducible mini-puppet pattern to cut out and color.

(front)

Letter formation activity

Beginning sounds activity

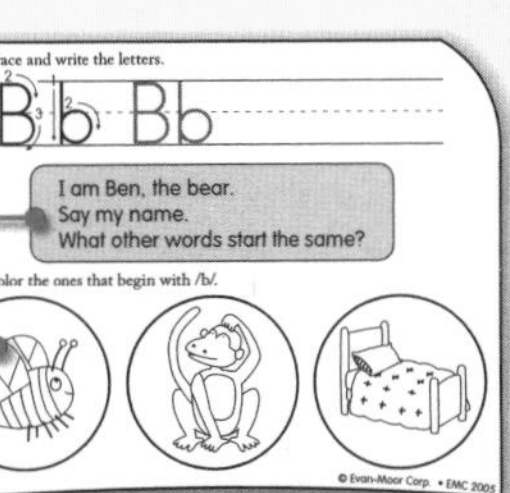

(back)

Picture Cards

The six colorful picture cards included for each letter:

- teach matching beginning sounds,
- engage students in practicing letter-sound recognition, and
- can be used as a tool for assessing student proficiency. (Mix cards from all letters together and ask a student to place each card with the puppet that has the same beginning sound.)

bed
baby
bee
bat
boat
basket

Teacher's Guide

Five easy teaching steps are suggested for each letter:

1. Introduce the letter and its sound.
2. Practice letter formation.
3. Support letter recognition by sight and sound.
4. Teach letters as initial sounds.
5. Review concepts.

Use these steps in sequence to introduce one letter at a time, or focus on just one or two steps to introduce several letters at a time.

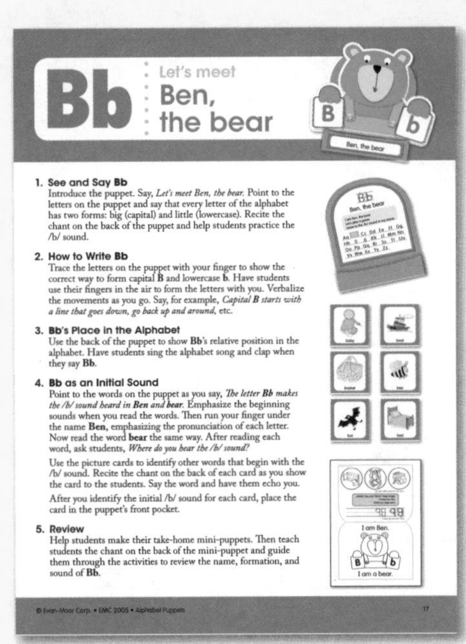

Bb Let's meet **Ben, the bear**

1. **See and Say Bb**
Introduce the puppet. Say, *Let's meet Ben, the bear.* Point to the letters on the puppet and say that every letter of the alphabet has two forms: big (capital) and little (lowercase). Recite the chant on the back of the puppet and help students practice the /b/ sound.

2. **How to Write Bb**
Trace the letters on the puppet with your finger to show the correct way to form capital **B** and lowercase **b**. Have students use their fingers in the air to form the letters with you. Verbalize the movements as you go. Say, for example, *Capital **B** starts with a line that goes down, go back up and around,* etc.

3. **Bb's Place in the Alphabet**
Use the back of the puppet to show **Bb**'s relative position in the alphabet. Have students sing the alphabet song and clap when they say **Bb**.

4. **Bb as an Initial Sound**
Point to the words on the puppet as you say, *The letter **Bb** makes the /b/ sound heard in **Ben** and **bear**.* Emphasize the beginning sounds when you read the words. Then run your finger under the name **Ben,** emphasizing the pronunciation of each letter. Now read the word **bear** the same way. After reading each word, ask students, *Where do you hear the /b/ sound?*

   Use the picture cards to identify other words that begin with the /b/ sound. Recite the chant on the back of each card as you show the card to the students. Say the word and have them echo you.

   After you identify the initial /b/ sound for each card, place the card in the puppet's front pocket.

5. **Review**
Help students make their take-home mini-puppets. Then teach students the chant on the back of the mini-puppet and guide them through the activities to review the name, formation, and sound of **Bb**.

© Evan-Moor Corp. • EMC 2005 • Alphabet Puppets

Games to Play

You can invent any number of games to play with the alphabet puppets and picture cards. Here are some suggestions to get you started:

Puppets Only

Put Them in Order

Practice alphabetical order by asking students to work together to put the puppets in correct alphabetical order. Increase the difficulty of this game by hiding one of the puppets and letting the students discover which letter is missing.

A Few of My Favorite Things

Have each student pick a favorite puppet. Then have them each make a list of their puppet's favorite things and share the list with the class. All the items on the list must begin with the same sound as the puppet's name. *I am Ben, the bear. I like bugs, baskets, bananas….*

Puppets and Cards

"It's Mine!"

Let five students each pick a puppet. Hold up a picture card and say the word. The student who has the puppet with the matching beginning sound should call out, *"It's mine."* If the card doesn't belong to anyone, place it in a discard pile.

Deliver the Cards

Place three puppets on a table. Mix up the picture cards for those puppets and ask a student to "deliver" each card to the correct puppet. The student should place each card in the front pocket of the puppet with the same beginning sound and then ask another child to check his or her work.

Cards Only

Which One Is Different?

Place five picture cards on a table. Four of the cards should have the same beginning sound. Ask students to find the one that is different. Increase the difficulty of this game by adding more cards.

Which Ones Are the Same?

Place five picture cards on a table. Make sure that two of the cards have the same beginning sound. The other three cards should each have a different beginning sound. Ask students to find the two cards with the same beginning sound.

Puppet Mitt Template

You will need:
construction paper scissors stapler* glue

(front)
(back)

1. Photocopy this page and cut out the copy of the mitt template. Lay it on 2 sheets of 9" x 12" (23 x 30.5 cm) construction paper and cut around the shape.

2. Fold up 1½" (4 cm) at the bottom of each construction paper shape. Fold one piece to the front; fold the other piece to the back *(as shown)*. Staple the two pieces of the mitt together. Staple only around the top and side edges *(as shown)*. Leave the bottom of the mitt open.

* If you prefer, you can use glue or double-sided tape, instead of a stapler, to hold the mitt together.

3. Glue the puppet character and its name onto the front of the mitt. Glue the chant and alphabet chart onto the back.

4. Cut out the picture cards. Store them in the pocket on the back of the puppet.

Now the puppet is ready to use!

fold

1½"

Alphabet Song

Traditional Children's Song

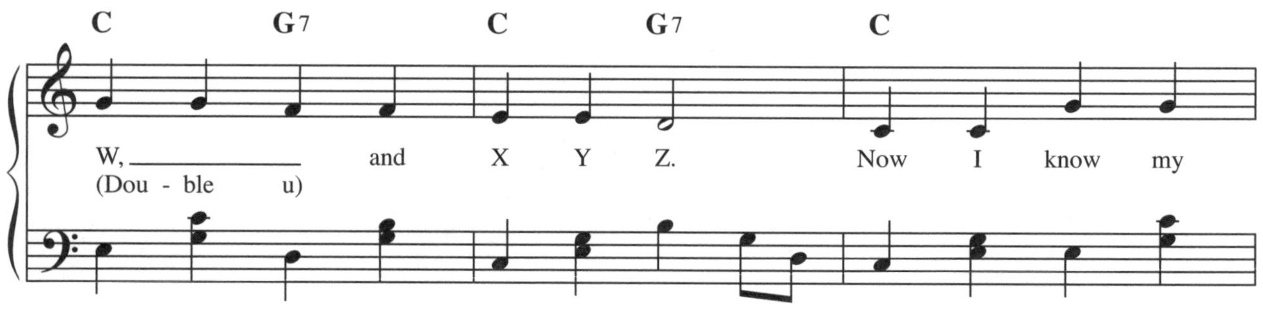

Let's meet Andy, the ant

1. **See and Say Aa**
   Introduce the puppet. Say, *Let's meet Andy, the ant.* Point to the letters on the puppet and say that every letter of the alphabet has two forms: big (capital) and little (lowercase). Recite the chant on the back of the puppet and help students practice the short **a** sound.

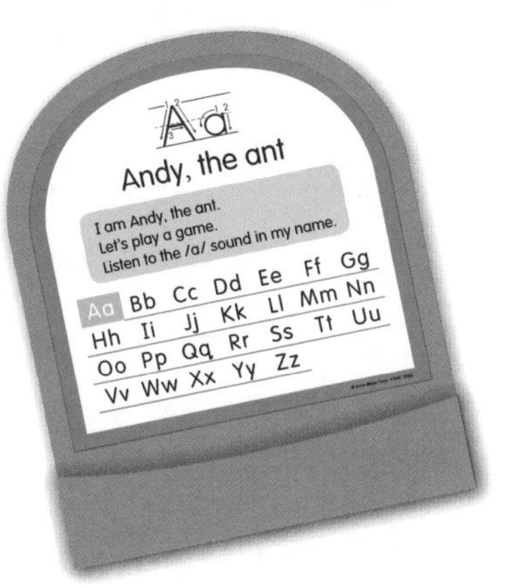

2. **How to Write Aa**
   Trace the letters on the puppet with your finger to show the correct way to form capital **A** and lowercase **a**. Have students use their fingers in the air to form the letters with you. Verbalize the movements as you go. Say, for example, *Capital A starts at the top and goes down, back to the top and down*, etc.

3. **Aa's Place in the Alphabet**
   Use the back of the puppet to show **Aa**'s relative position in the alphabet. Have students sing the alphabet song and clap when they say **Aa**.

/a/ /ā/

4. **Short Aa as an Initial Sound**
   Point to the words on the puppet as you say, *Sometimes, the letter **Aa** makes the /a/ sound heard in **Andy** and **ant**.* Emphasize the beginning sounds when you read the words. Then run your finger under the name **Andy**, emphasizing the pronunciation of each letter. Now read the word **ant** the same way. After reading each word, ask students, *Where do you hear the /a/ sound?*

   Use the picture cards to identify other words that begin with the /a/ sound. Recite the chant on the back of each card as you show the card to the students. Say the word and have them echo you.

   Place the three cards that show /a/ (short **a**) words in the puppet's front pocket. Save the three cards with /ā/ (long **a**) words to introduce later. *(See page 218.)*

5. **Review**
   Help students make their take-home mini-puppets. Then teach students the chant on the back of the mini-puppet and guide them through the activities to review the name, formation, and sound of **Aa**.

Trace and write the letters.

A a A a

I am Andy, the ant.
Say my name.
What other words start the same?

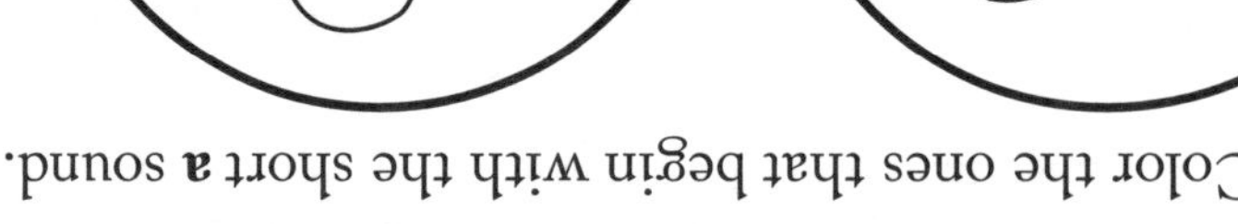

Color the ones that begin with the short **a** sound.

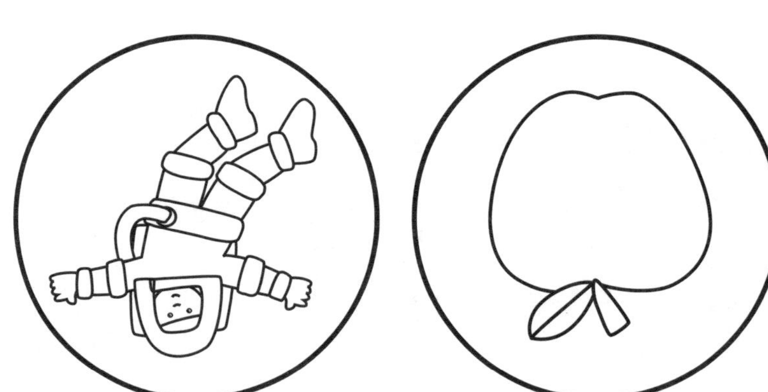

fold

I am Andy.

I am an ant.

Note: Cut along dashed lines. Glue figure to front of construction paper mitt, above the pocket. *(See page 7 for mitt template and instructions.)*

Note: Cut along dashed lines. Glue name strip across front pocket of construction paper mitt. Glue rhyme and alphabet chart to back of mitt, above the pocket.
(See page 7 for mitt template and instructions.)

Andy, the ant

I am Andy, the ant.
Let's play a game.
Listen to the /a/ sound in my name.

Aa	Bb	Cc	Dd	Ee	Ff	Gg
Hh	Ii	Jj	Kk	Ll	Mm	Nn
Oo	Pp	Qq	Rr	Ss	Tt	Uu
Vv	Ww	Xx	Yy	Zz		

Andy, the ant

astronaut

alligator

apple

apron

acorn

angel

Look at Andy, the ant.
Think of his name.
What other word
starts the same?

Look at Andy, the ant.
Think of his name.
What other word
starts the same?

Look at Andy, the ant.
Think of his name.
What other word
starts the same?

Look at Amy, the ant.
Think of her name.
What other word
starts the same?

Look at Amy, the ant.
Think of her name.
What other word
starts the same?

Look at Amy, the ant.
Think of her name.
What other word
starts the same?

Bb Let's meet Ben, the bear

1. See and Say Bb

Introduce the puppet. Say, *Let's meet Ben, the bear.* Point to the letters on the puppet and say that every letter of the alphabet has two forms: big (capital) and little (lowercase). Recite the chant on the back of the puppet and help students practice the /b/ sound.

2. How to Write Bb

Trace the letters on the puppet with your finger to show the correct way to form capital **B** and lowercase **b**. Have students use their fingers in the air to form the letters with you. Verbalize the movements as you go. Say, for example, *Capital **B** starts with a line that goes down, go back up and around,* etc.

3. Bb's Place in the Alphabet

Use the back of the puppet to show **Bb**'s relative position in the alphabet. Have students sing the alphabet song and clap when they say **Bb**.

4. Bb as an Initial Sound

Point to the words on the puppet as you say, *The letter **Bb** makes the /b/ sound heard in **Ben** and **bear**.* Emphasize the beginning sounds when you read the words. Then run your finger under the name **Ben**, emphasizing the pronunciation of each letter. Now read the word **bear** the same way. After reading each word, ask students, *Where do you hear the /b/ sound?*

Use the picture cards to identify other words that begin with the /b/ sound. Recite the chant on the back of each card as you show the card to the students. Say the word and have them echo you.

After you identify the initial /b/ sound for each card, place the card in the puppet's front pocket.

5. Review

Help students make their take-home mini-puppets. Then teach students the chant on the back of the mini-puppet and guide them through the activities to review the name, formation, and sound of **Bb**.

fold

I am Ben.

I am a bear.

Trace and write the letters.

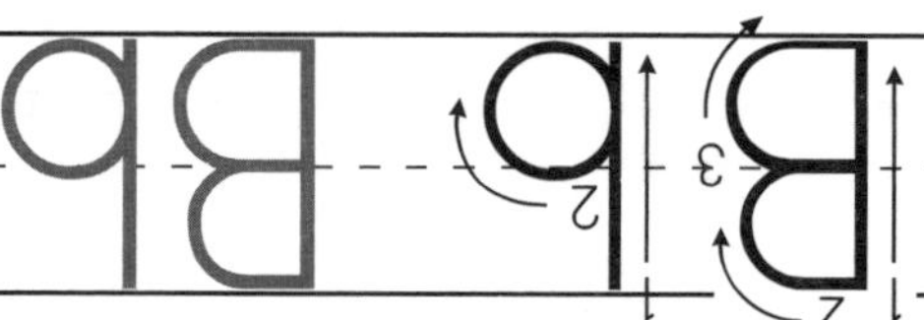

I am Ben, the bear.
Say my name.
What other words start the same?

Color the ones that begin with /b/.

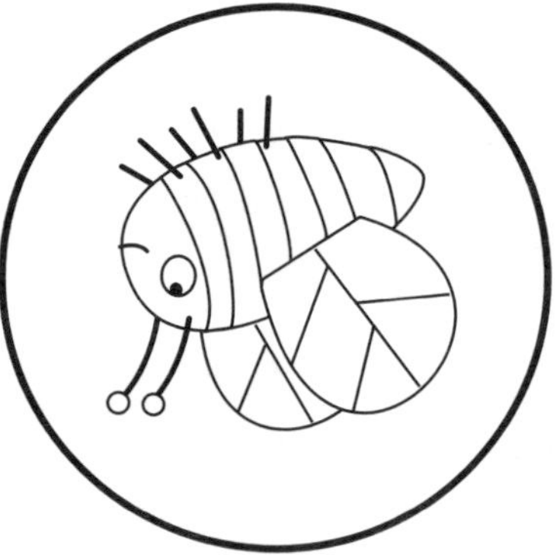

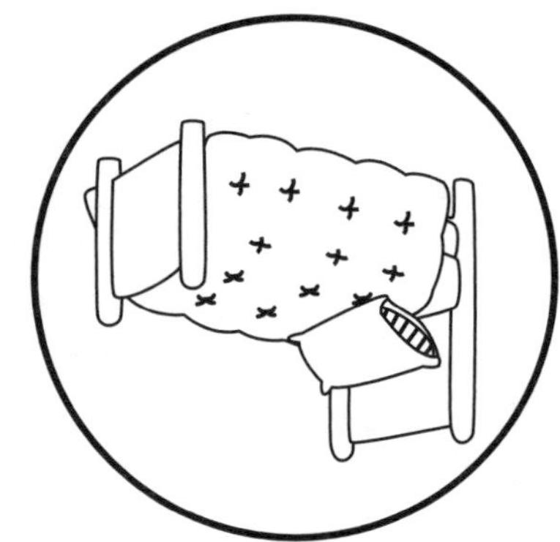

Note: Cut along dashed lines. Glue figure to front of construction paper mitt, above the pocket. *(See page 7 for mitt template and instructions.)*

Note: Cut along dashed lines. Glue name strip across front pocket of construction paper mitt. Glue rhyme and alphabet chart to back of mitt, above the pocket. *(See page 7 for mitt template and instructions.)*

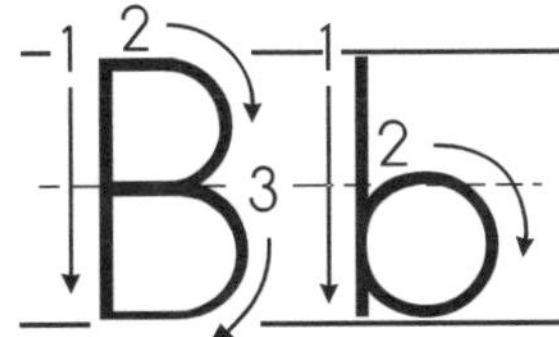

Ben, the bear

I am Ben, the bear.
Let's play a game.
Listen to the /b/ sound in my name.

Aa Bb Cc Dd Ee Ff Gg
Hh Ii Jj Kk Ll Mm Nn
Oo Pp Qq Rr Ss Tt Uu
Vv Ww Xx Yy Zz

Ben, the bear

bat

basket

baby

bed

bee

boat

Look at Ben, the bear.
Think of his name.
What other word
starts the same?

Look at Ben, the bear.
Think of his name.
What other word
starts the same?

© Evan-Moor Corp. • EMC 2005

Look at Ben, the bear.
Think of his name.
What other word
starts the same?

© Evan-Moor Corp. • EMC 2005

Look at Ben, the bear.
Think of his name.
What other word
starts the same?

© Evan-Moor Corp. • EMC 2005

Look at Ben, the bear.
Think of his name.
What other word
starts the same?

© Evan-Moor Corp. • EMC 2005

Look at Ben, the bear.
Think of his name.
What other word
starts the same?

© Evan-Moor Corp. • EMC 2005

Cc Let's meet Callie, the cat

1. **See and Say Cc**
   Introduce the puppet. Say, *Let's meet Callie, the cat.* Point to the letters on the puppet and say that every letter of the alphabet has two forms: big (capital) and little (lowercase). Recite the chant on the back of the puppet and help students practice the /k/ sound.

2. **How to Write Cc**
   Trace the letters on the puppet with your finger to show the correct way to form capital **C** and lowercase **c**. Have students use their fingers in the air to form the letters with you. Verbalize the movements as you go. Say, for example, *Capital **C** starts at the top and curves back, around, and down,* etc.

3. **Cc's Place in the Alphabet**
   Use the back of the puppet to show **Cc**'s relative position in the alphabet. Have students sing the alphabet song and clap when they say **Cc**.

4. **Cc as an Initial Sound**
   Point to the words on the puppet as you say, *The letter **Cc** makes the /k/ sound heard in **Callie** and **cat**.* Emphasize the beginning sound when you say the words. Then run your finger under the name **Callie**, emphasizing the pronunciation of each letter. Now read the word **cat** the same way. After reading each word, ask students, *Where do you hear the /k/ sound?*

   Use the picture cards to identify other words that begin with the /k/ sound. Recite the chant on the back of each card as you show the card to the students. Say the word and have them echo you.

   After you identify the initial /k/ sound for each card, place the card in the puppet's front pocket.

5. **Review**
   Help students make their take-home mini-puppets. Then teach students the chant on the back of the mini-puppet and guide them through the activities to review the name, formation, and sound of **Cc**.

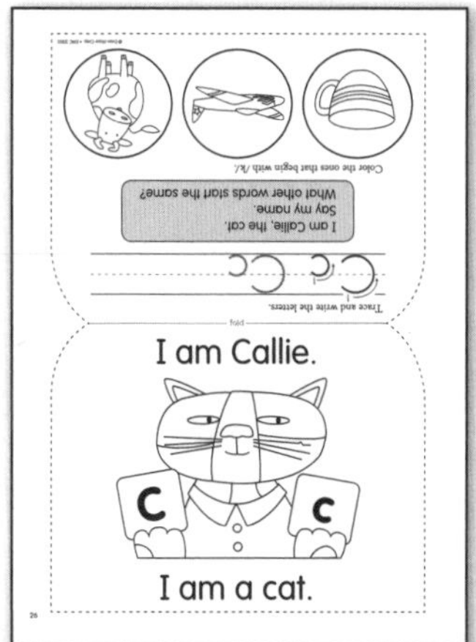

Trace and write the letters.

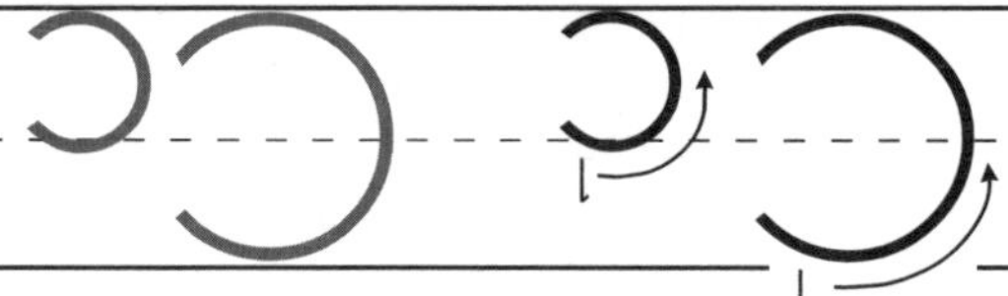

I am Callie, the cat.
Say my name.
What other words start the same?

Color the ones that begin with /k/.

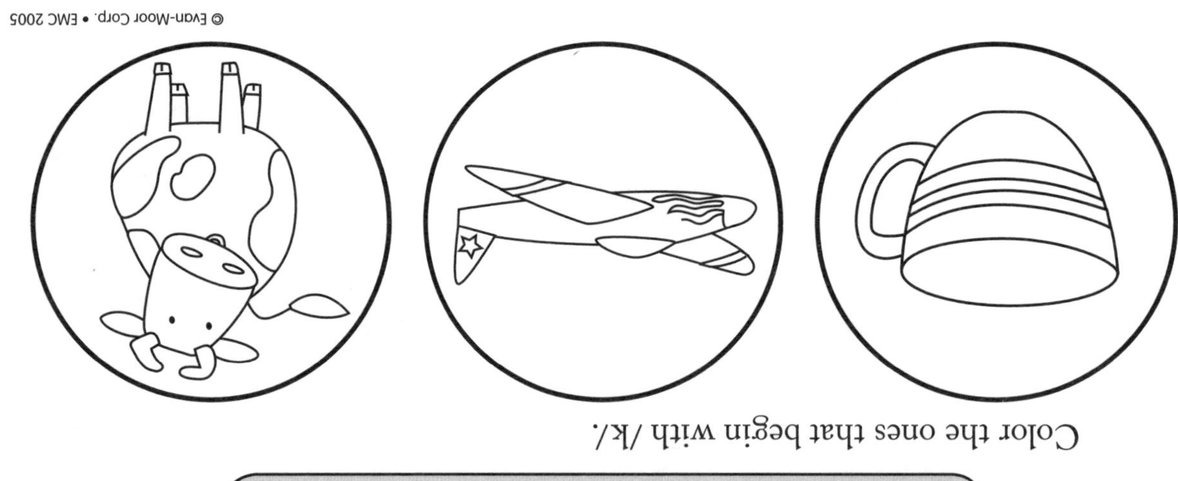

fold

I am Callie.

I am a cat.

Note: Cut along dashed lines. Glue figure to front of construction paper mitt, above the pocket. *(See page 7 for mitt template and instructions.)*

Note: Cut along dashed lines. Glue name strip across front pocket of construction paper mitt. Glue rhyme and alphabet chart to back of mitt, above the pocket. *(See page 7 for mitt template and instructions.)*

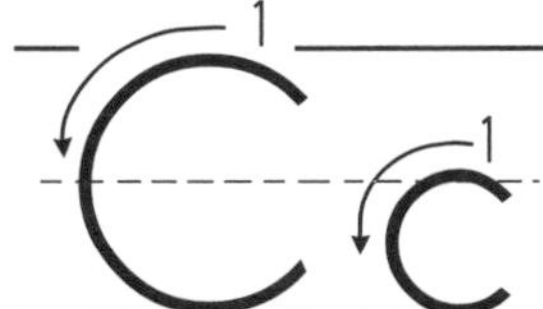

Callie, the cat

I am Callie, the cat.
Let's play a game.
Listen to the /k/ sound in my name.

Aa	Bb	Cc	Dd	Ee	Ff	Gg
Hh	Ii	Jj	Kk	Ll	Mm	Nn
Oo	Pp	Qq	Rr	Ss	Tt	Uu
Vv	Ww	Xx	Yy	Zz		

Callie, the cat

candle

can

cake

cup

cow

corn

Look at Callie, the cat.
Think of her name.
What other word
starts the same?

Look at Callie, the cat.
Think of her name.
What other word
starts the same?

Look at Callie, the cat.
Think of her name.
What other word
starts the same?

Look at Callie, the cat.
Think of her name.
What other word
starts the same?

Look at Callie, the cat.
Think of her name.
What other word
starts the same?

Look at Callie, the cat.
Think of her name.
What other word
starts the same?

Dd Let's meet Digger, the dog

1. **See and Say Dd**
   Introduce the puppet. Say, *Let's meet Digger, the dog.* Point to the letters on the puppet and say that every letter of the alphabet has two forms: big (capital) and little (lowercase). Recite the chant on the back of the puppet and help students practice the /d/ sound.

2. **How to Write Dd**
   Trace the letters on the puppet with your finger to show the correct way to form capital **D** and lowercase **d**. Have students use their fingers in the air to form the letters with you. Verbalize the movements as you go. Say, for example, *Capital **D** starts with a stick, go back to the top and curve down,* etc.

3. **Dd's Place in the Alphabet**
   Use the back of the puppet to show **Dd**'s relative position in the alphabet. Have students sing the alphabet song and clap when they say **Dd**.

4. **Dd as an Initial Sound**
   Point to the words on the puppet as you say, *The letter **Dd** makes the /d/ sound heard in **Digger** and **dog**.* Emphasize the beginning sound when you say the words. Then run your finger under the name **Digger**, emphasizing the pronunciation of each letter. Now read the word **dog** the same way. After reading each word, ask students, *Where do you hear the /d/ sound?*

   Use the picture cards to identify other words that begin with the /d/ sound. Recite the chant on the back of each card as you show the card to the students. Say the word and have them echo you.

   After you identify the initial /d/ sound for each card, place the card in the puppet's front pocket.

5. **Review**
   Help students make their take-home mini-puppets. Then teach students the chant on the back of the mini-puppet and guide them through the activities to review the name, formation, and sound of **Dd**.

Trace and write the letters.

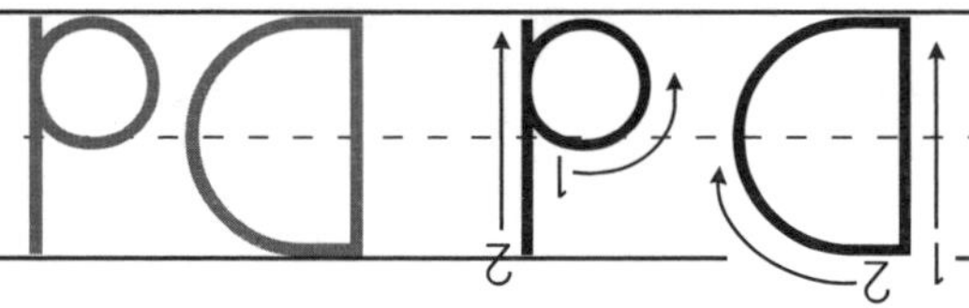

I am Digger, the dog.
Say my name.
What other words start the same?

Color the ones that begin with /d/.

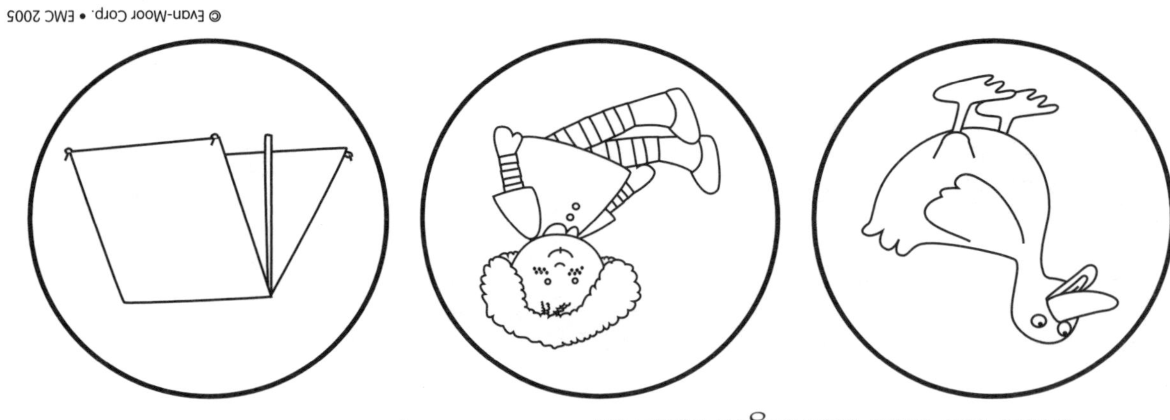

fold

I am Digger.

I am a dog.

Note: Cut along dashed lines. Glue figure to front of construction paper mitt, above the pocket. *(See page 7 for mitt template and instructions.)*

Note: Cut along dashed lines. Glue name strip across front pocket of construction paper mitt. Glue rhyme and alphabet chart to back of mitt, above the pocket. *(See page 7 for mitt template and instructions.)*

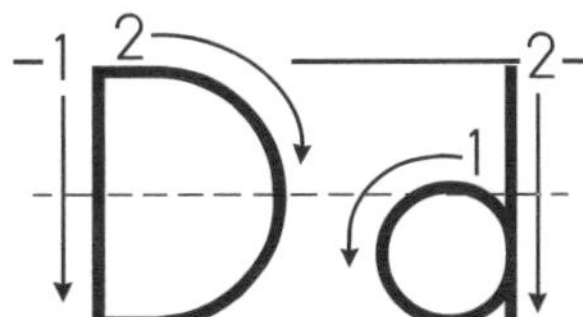

Digger, the dog

I am Digger, the dog.
Let's play a game.
Listen to the /d/ sound in my name.

Aa Bb Cc **Dd** Ee Ff Gg
Hh Ii Jj Kk Ll Mm Nn
Oo Pp Qq Rr Ss Tt Uu
Vv Ww Xx Yy Zz

Digger, the dog

doctor

dinosaur

deer

duck

door

doll

Look at Digger, the dog.
Think of his name.
What other word
starts the same?

Look at Digger, the dog.
Think of his name.
What other word
starts the same?

© Evan-Moor Corp. • EMC 2005

Look at Digger, the dog.
Think of his name.
What other word
starts the same?

© Evan-Moor Corp. • EMC 2005

Look at Digger, the dog.
Think of his name.
What other word
starts the same?

© Evan-Moor Corp. • EMC 2005

Look at Digger, the dog.
Think of his name.
What other word
starts the same?

© Evan-Moor Corp. • EMC 2005

Look at Digger, the dog.
Think of his name.
What other word
starts the same?

© Evan-Moor Corp. • EMC 2005

Ee Let's meet Elmo, the elephant

1. **See and Say Ee**
   Introduce the puppet. Say, *Let's meet Elmo, the elephant.* Point to the letters on the puppet and say that every letter of the alphabet has two forms: big (capital) and little (lowercase). Recite the chant on the back of the puppet and help students practice the short **e** sound.

2. **How to Write Ee**
   Trace the letters on the puppet with your finger to show the correct way to form capital **E** and lowercase **e**. Have students use their fingers in the air to form the letters with you. Verbalize the movements as you go. Say, for example, *Capital **E** starts at the top, draw a line down, back to the top, draw a line across,* etc.

/e/ /ē/

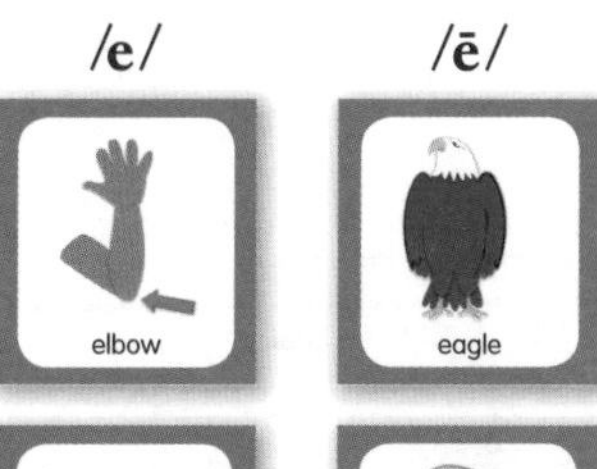

3. **Ee's Place in the Alphabet**
   Use the back of the puppet to show **Ee**'s relative position in the alphabet. Have students sing the alphabet song and clap when they say **Ee**.

4. **Short Ee as an Initial Sound**
   Point to the words on the puppet as you say, *Sometimes, the letter **Ee** makes the /e/ sound heard in **Elmo** and **elephant**.* Emphasize the beginning sound when you say the words. Then run your finger under the name **Elmo**, emphasizing the pronunciation of each letter. Now read the word **elephant** the same way. After reading each word, ask students, *Where do you hear the /e/ sound?*

   Use the picture cards to identify other words that begin with the /e/ sound. Recite the chant on the back of each card as you show the card to the students. Say the word and have them echo you.

   Place the three cards that show /e/ (short **e**) words in the puppet's front pocket. Save the three cards with /ē/ (long **e**) words to introduce later. *(See page 218.)*

5. **Review**
   Help students make their take-home mini-puppets. Then teach students the chant on the back of the mini-puppet and guide them through the activities to review the name, formation, and sound of **Ee**.

Trace and write the letters.

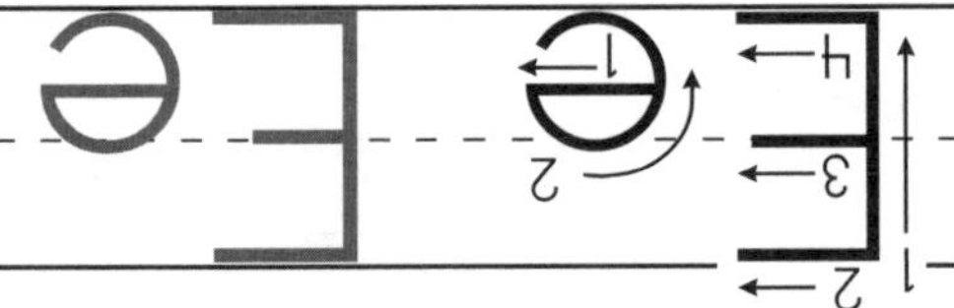

I am Elmo, the elephant.
Say my name.
What other words start the same?

Color the ones that begin with the short **e** sound.

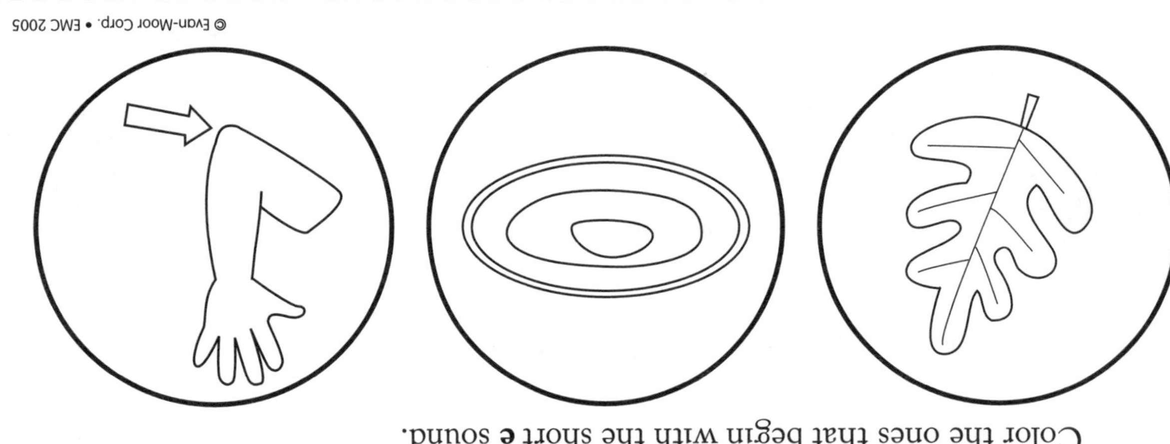

fold

I am Elmo.

I am an elephant.

Note: Cut along dashed lines. Glue figure to front of construction paper mitt, above the pocket.
(See page 7 for mitt template and instructions.)

Note: Cut along dashed lines. Glue name strip across front pocket of construction paper mitt. Glue rhyme and alphabet chart to back of mitt, above the pocket. *(See page 7 for mitt template and instructions.)*

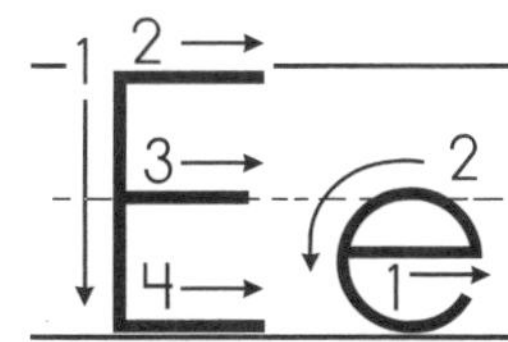

Elmo, the elephant

I am Elmo, the elephant.
Let's play a game.
Listen to the /e/ sound in my name.

Aa Bb Cc Dd Ee Ff Gg
Hh Ii Jj Kk Ll Mm Nn
Oo Pp Qq Rr Ss Tt Uu
Vv Ww Xx Yy Zz

Elmo, the elephant

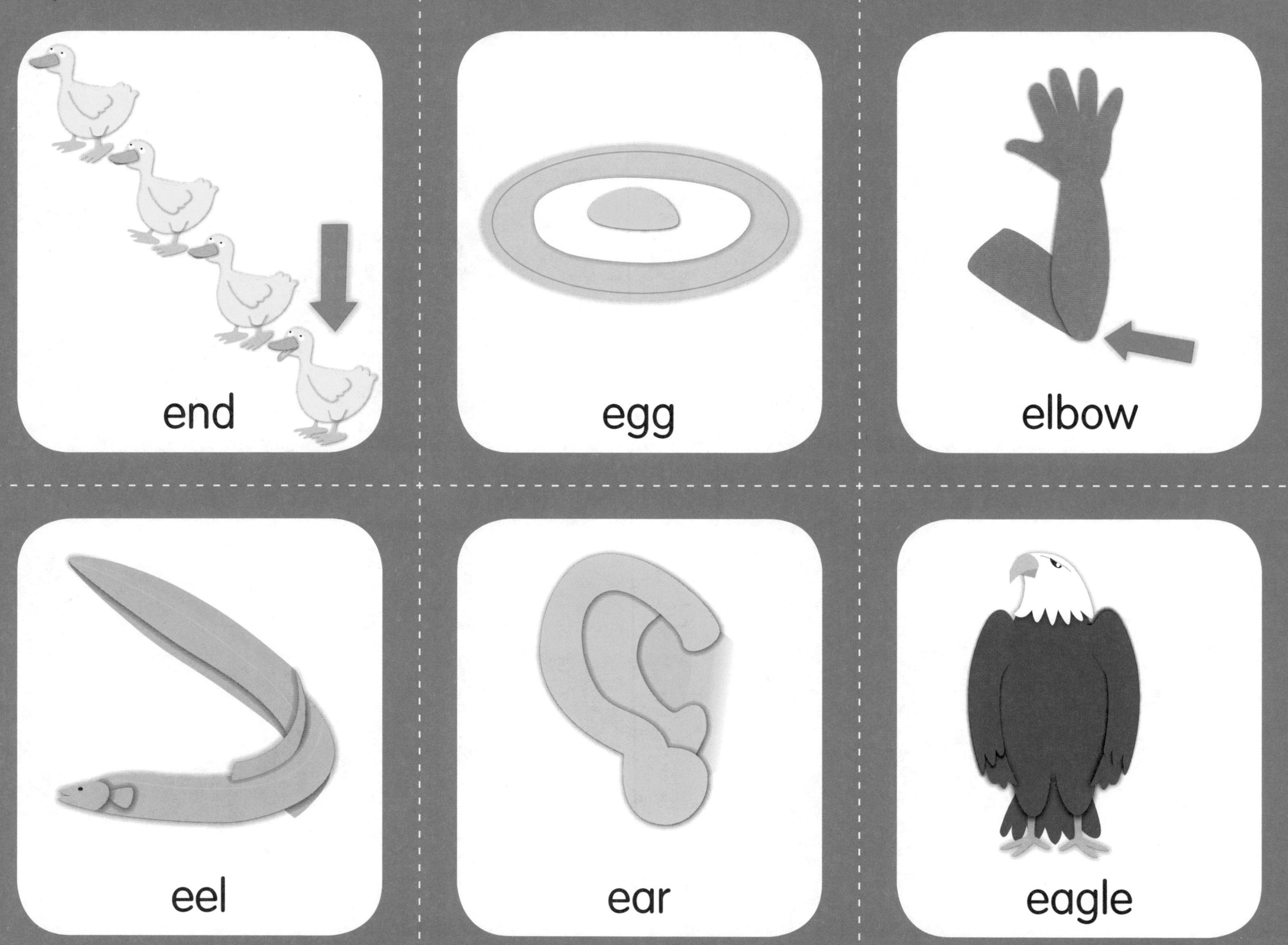
end
egg
elbow
eel
ear
eagle

Look at Elmo, the elephant.
Think of his name.
What other word
starts the same?

Look at Elmo, the elephant.
Think of his name.
What other word
starts the same?

Look at Elmo, the elephant.
Think of his name.
What other word
starts the same?

Look at Eva, the elephant.
Think of her name.
What other word
starts the same?

Look at Eva, the elephant.
Think of her name.
What other word
starts the same?

Look at Eva, the elephant.
Think of her name.
What other word
starts the same?

Ff Let's meet Finny, the fish

1. See and Say Ff

Introduce the puppet. Say, *Let's meet Finny, the fish.* Point to the letters on the puppet and say that every letter of the alphabet has two forms: big (capital) and little (lowercase). Recite the chant on the back of the puppet and help students practice the /f/ sound.

2. How to Write Ff

Trace the letters on the puppet with your finger to show the correct way to form capital **F** and lowercase **f**. Have students use their fingers in the air to form the letters with you. Verbalize the movements as you go. Say, for example, *Capital **F** starts at the top, draw a stick down, and add two lines across,* etc.

3. Ff's Place in the Alphabet

Use the back of the puppet to show **Ff**'s relative position in the alphabet. Have students sing the alphabet song and clap when they say **Ff**.

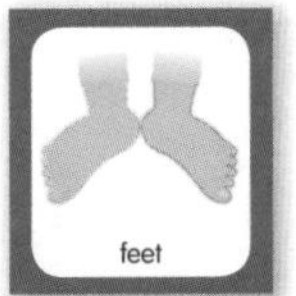

4. Ff as an Initial Sound

Point to the words on the puppet as you say, *The letter **Ff** makes the /f/ sound heard in **Finny** and **fish**.* Emphasize the beginning sound when you say the words. Then run your finger under the name **Finny**, emphasizing the pronunciation of each letter. Now read the word **fish** the same way. After reading each word, ask students, *Where do you hear the /f/ sound?*

Use the picture cards to identify other words that begin with the /f/ sound. Recite the chant on the back of each card as you show the card to the students. Say the word and have them echo you.

After you identify the initial /f/ sound for each card, place the card in the puppet's front pocket.

5. Review

Help students make their take-home mini-puppets. Then teach students the chant on the back of the mini-puppet and guide them through the activities to review the name, formation, and sound of **Ff**.

Trace and write the letters.

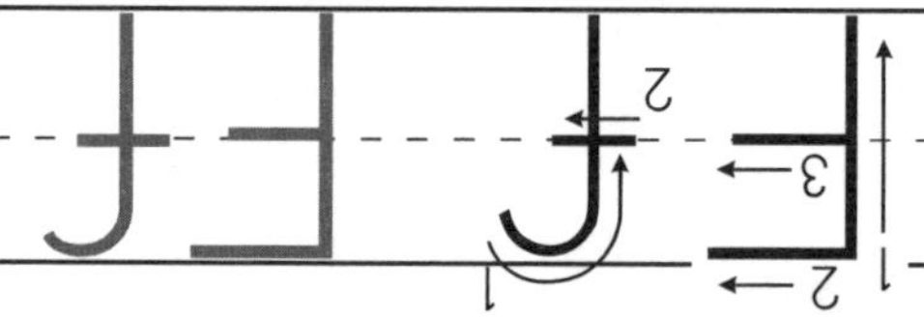

I am Finny, the fish.
Say my name.
What other words start the same?

Color the ones that begin with /f/.

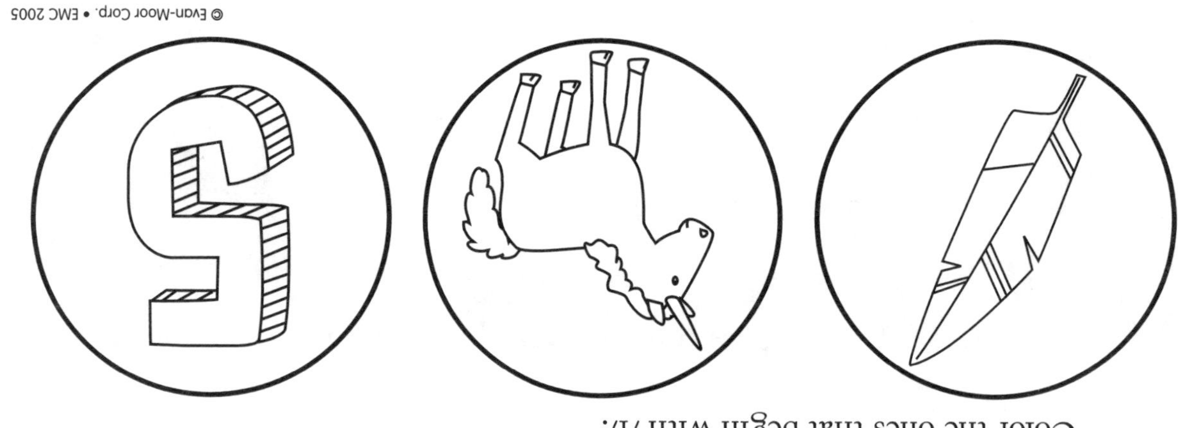

fold

I am Finny.

I am a fish.

Note: Cut along dashed lines. Glue figure to front of construction paper mitt, above the pocket. *(See page 7 for mitt template and instructions.)*

Note: Cut along dashed lines. Glue name strip across front pocket of construction paper mitt. Glue rhyme and alphabet chart to back of mitt, above the pocket. *(See page 7 for mitt template and instructions.)*

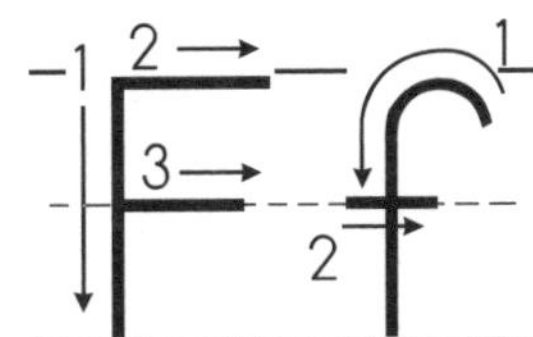

Finny, the fish

I am Finny, the fish.
Let's play a game.
Listen to the /f/ sound in my name.

Aa	Bb	Cc	Dd	Ee	Ff	Gg
Hh	Ii	Jj	Kk	Ll	Mm	Nn
Oo	Pp	Qq	Rr	Ss	Tt	Uu
Vv	Ww	Xx	Yy	Zz		

Finny, the fish

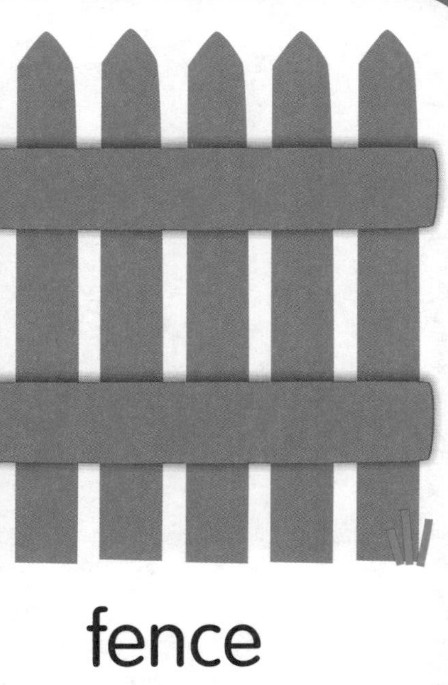

fence

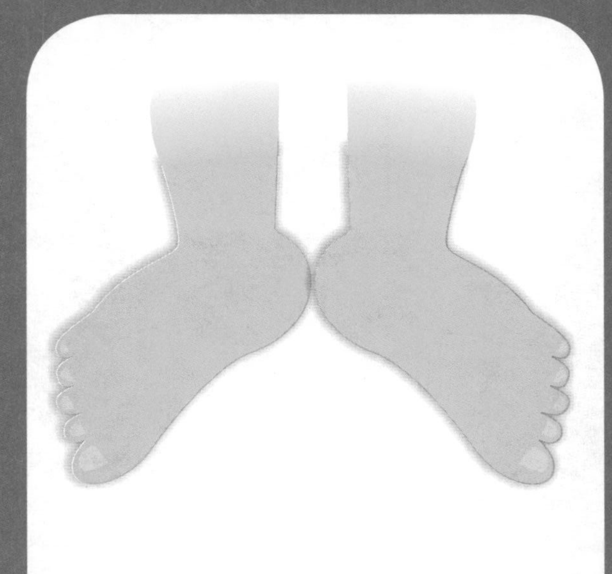

feet

feather

fox

five

fire

Look at Finny, the fish.
Think of his name.
What other word
starts the same?

Look at Finny, the fish.
Think of his name.
What other word
starts the same?

© Evan-Moor Corp. • EMC 2005

Look at Finny, the fish.
Think of his name.
What other word
starts the same?

© Evan-Moor Corp. • EMC 2005

Look at Finny, the fish.
Think of his name.
What other word
starts the same?

© Evan-Moor Corp. • EMC 2005

Look at Finny, the fish.
Think of his name.
What other word
starts the same?

© Evan-Moor Corp. • EMC 2005

Look at Finny, the fish.
Think of his name.
What other word
starts the same?

© Evan-Moor Corp. • EMC 2005

Gg Let's meet Gerty, the gorilla

1. **See and Say Gg**
   Introduce the puppet. Say, *Let's meet Gerty, the gorilla.* Point to the letters on the puppet and say that every letter of the alphabet has two forms: big (capital) and little (lowercase). Recite the chant on the back of the puppet and help students practice the /g/ sound.

2. **How to Write Gg**
   Trace the letters on the puppet with your finger to show the correct way to form capital **G** and lowercase **g**. Have students use their fingers in the air to form the letters with you. Verbalize the movements as you go. Say, for example, *Capital* ***G*** *starts at the top and curves around,* etc.

3. **Gg's Place in the Alphabet**
   Use the back of the puppet to show **Gg**'s relative position in the alphabet. Have students sing the alphabet song and clap when they say **Gg**.

4. **Gg as an Initial Sound**
   Point to the words on the puppet as you say, *The letter* ***Gg*** *makes the /g/ sound heard in* ***Gerty*** *and* ***gorilla***. Emphasize the beginning sound when you say the words. Then run your finger under the name **Gerty**, emphasizing the pronunciation of each letter. Now read the word **gorilla** the same way. After reading each word, ask students, *Where do you hear the /g/ sound?*

   Use the picture cards to identify other words that begin with the /g/ sound. Recite the chant on the back of each card as you show the card to the students. Say the word and have them echo you.

   After you identify the initial /g/ sound for each card, place the card in the puppet's front pocket.

5. **Review**
   Help students make their take-home mini-puppets. Then teach students the chant on the back of the mini-puppet and guide them through the activities to review the name, formation, and sound of **Gg**.

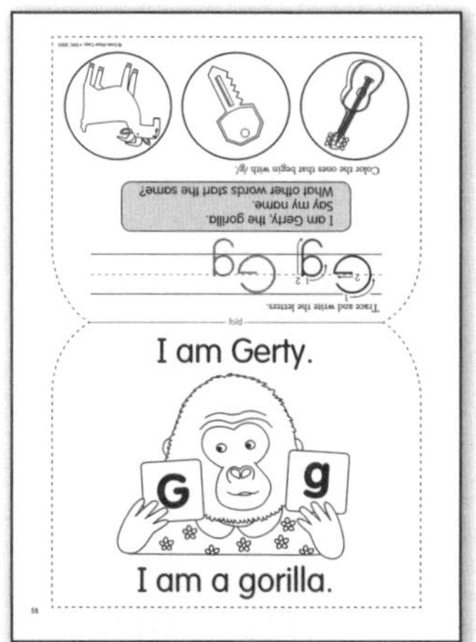

I am Gerty.

I am a gorilla.

fold

Trace and write the letters.

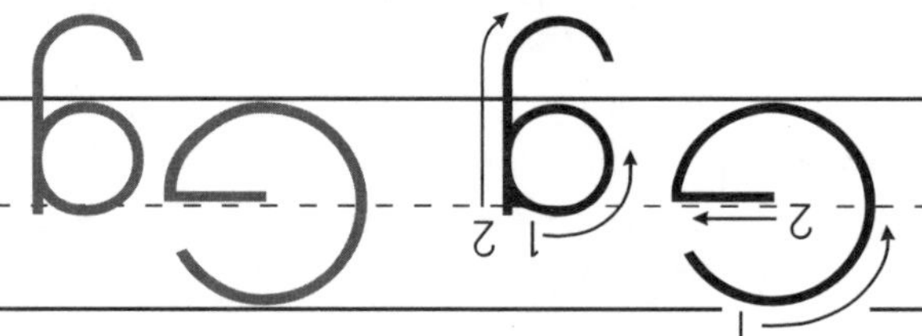

I am Gerty, the gorilla.
Say my name.
What other words start the same?

Color the ones that begin with /g/.

Note: Cut along dashed lines. Glue figure to front of construction paper mitt, above the pocket. *(See page 7 for mitt template and instructions.)*

g

G

Note: Cut along dashed lines. Glue name strip across front pocket of construction paper mitt. Glue rhyme and alphabet chart to back of mitt, above the pocket. *(See page 7 for mitt template and instructions.)*

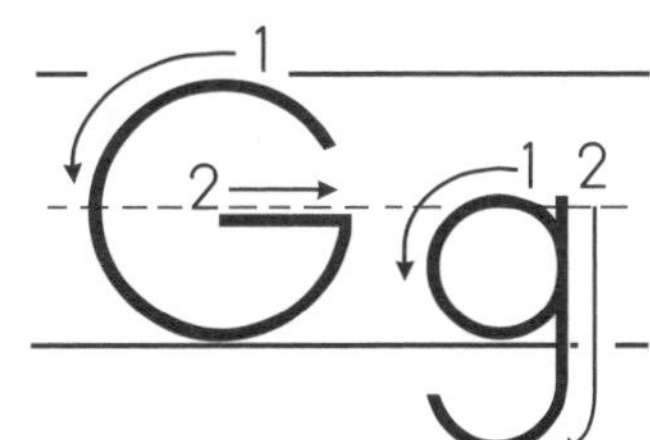

Gerty, the gorilla

I am Gerty, the gorilla.
Let's play a game.
Listen to the /g/ sound in my name.

Aa	Bb	Cc	Dd	Ee	Ff	Gg
Hh	Ii	Jj	Kk	Ll	Mm	Nn
Oo	Pp	Qq	Rr	Ss	Tt	Uu
Vv	Ww	Xx	Yy	Zz		

Gerty, the gorilla

girl
gate
garden
golf
guitar
goat

Look at Gerty, the gorilla.
Think of her name.
What other word
starts the same?

Look at Gerty, the gorilla.
Think of her name.
What other word
starts the same?

Look at Gerty, the gorilla.
Think of her name.
What other word
starts the same?

Look at Gerty, the gorilla.
Think of her name.
What other word
starts the same?

Look at Gerty, the gorilla.
Think of her name.
What other word
starts the same?

Look at Gerty, the gorilla.
Think of her name.
What other word
starts the same?

Hh Let's meet Hannah, the hen

1. **See and Say Hh**
   Introduce the puppet. Say, *Let's meet Hannah, the hen.* Point to the letters on the puppet and say that every letter of the alphabet has two forms: big (capital) and little (lowercase). Recite the chant on the back of the puppet and help students practice the /h/ sound.

2. **How to Write Hh**
   Trace the letters on the puppet with your finger to show the correct way to form capital **H** and lowercase **h**. Have students use their fingers in the air to form the letters with you. Verbalize the movements as you go. Say, for example, *Capital **H** starts with one stick down, and then another stick down, and add a bar across,* etc.

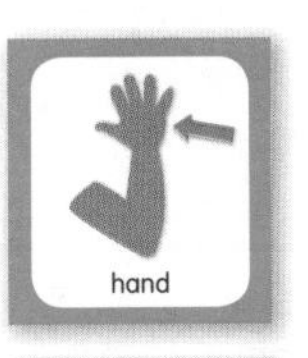

3. **Hh's Place in the Alphabet**
   Use the back of the puppet to show **Hh**'s relative position in the alphabet. Have students sing the alphabet song and clap when they say **Hh**.

4. **Hh as an Initial Sound**
   Point to the words on the puppet as you say, *The letter **Hh** makes the /h/ sound heard in **Hannah** and **hen**.* Emphasize the beginning sound when you say the words. Then run your finger under the name **Hannah**, emphasizing the pronunciation of each letter. Now read the word **hen** the same way. After reading each word, ask students, *Where do you hear the /h/ sound?*

   Use the picture cards to identify other words that begin with the /h/ sound. Recite the chant on the back of each card as you show the card to the students. Say the word and have them echo you.

   After you identify the initial /h/ sound for each card, place the card in the puppet's front pocket.

5. **Review**
   Help students make their take-home mini-puppets. Then teach students the chant on the back of the mini-puppet and guide them through the activities to review the name, formation, and sound of **Hh**.

Trace and write the letters.

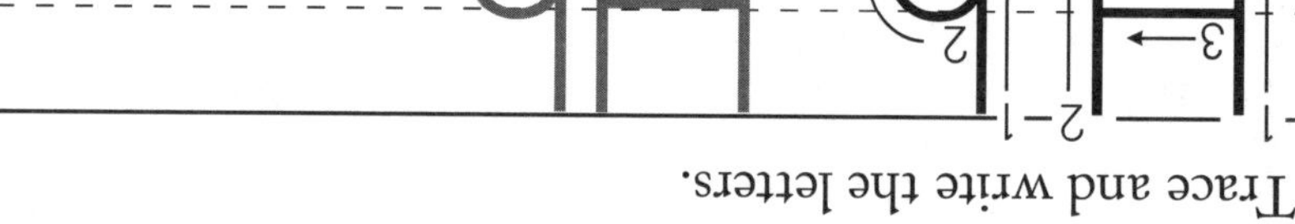

I am Hannah, the hen.
Say my name.
What other words start the same?

Color the ones that begin with /h/.

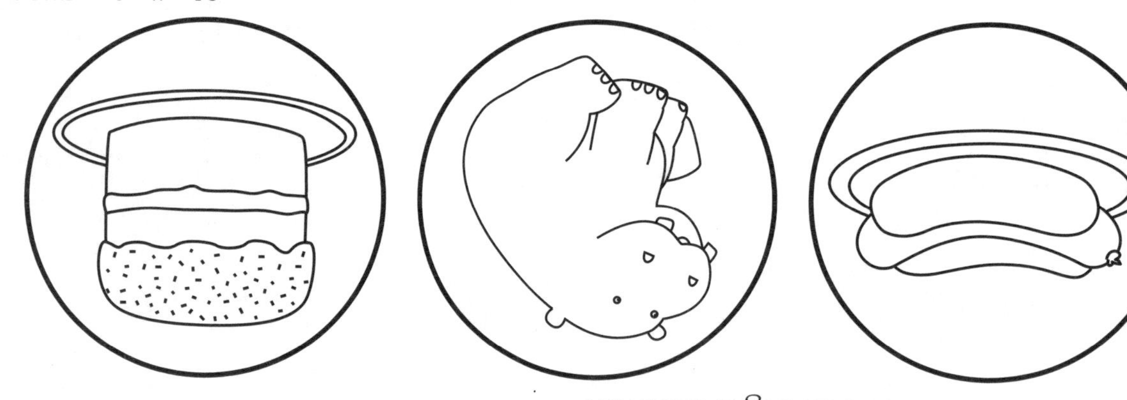

fold

I am Hannah.

I am a hen.

Note: Cut along dashed lines. Glue figure to front of construction paper mitt, above the pocket. *(See page 7 for mitt template and instructions.)*

Note: Cut along dashed lines. Glue name strip across front pocket of construction paper mitt. Glue rhyme and alphabet chart to back of mitt, above the pocket. *(See page 7 for mitt template and instructions.)*

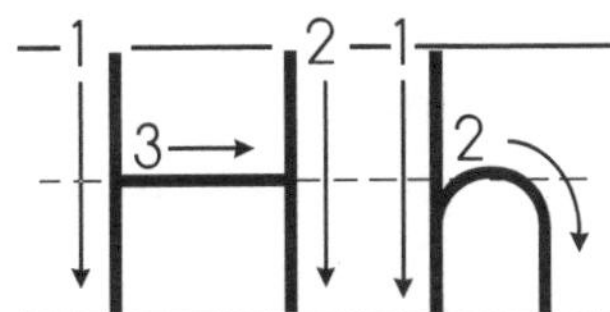

Hannah, the hen

I am Hannah, the hen.
Let's play a game.
Listen to the /h/ sound in my name.

Aa Bb Cc Dd Ee Ff Gg
Hh Ii Jj Kk Ll Mm Nn
Oo Pp Qq Rr Ss Tt Uu
Vv Ww Xx Yy Zz

Hannah, the hen

hippo

hat

hand

house

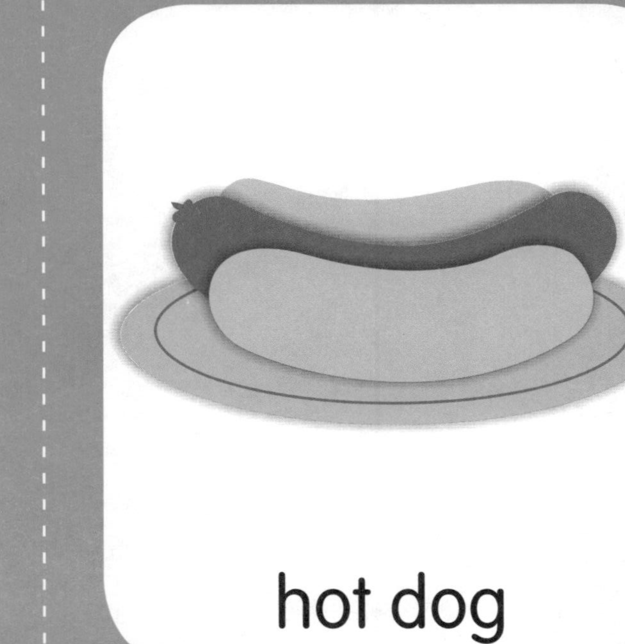

hot dog

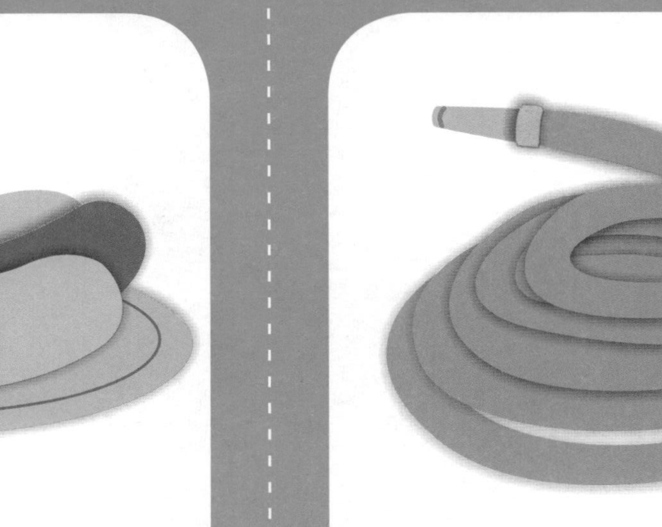

hose

Look at Hannah, the hen.
Think of her name.
What other word
starts the same?

Look at Hannah, the hen.
Think of her name.
What other word
starts the same?

Look at Hannah, the hen.
Think of her name.
What other word
starts the same?

Look at Hannah, the hen.
Think of her name.
What other word
starts the same?

Look at Hannah, the hen.
Think of her name.
What other word
starts the same?

Look at Hannah, the hen.
Think of her name.
What other word
starts the same?

Ii Let's meet Izzy, the iguana

1. See and Say Ii
Introduce the puppet. Say, *Let's meet Izzy, the iguana.* Point to the letters on the puppet and say that every letter of the alphabet has two forms: big (capital) and little (lowercase). Recite the chant on the back of the puppet and help students practice the short **i** sound.

2. How to Write Ii
Trace the letters on the puppet with your finger to show the correct way to form capital **I** and lowercase **i**. Have students use their fingers in the air to form the letters with you. Verbalize the movements as you go. Say, for example, *Capital **I** starts with a long stick down, then add a short line across the top and the bottom,* etc.

3. Ii's Place in the Alphabet
Use the back of the puppet to show **Ii**'s relative position in the alphabet. Have students sing the alphabet song and clap when they say **Ii**.

/i/ /ī/

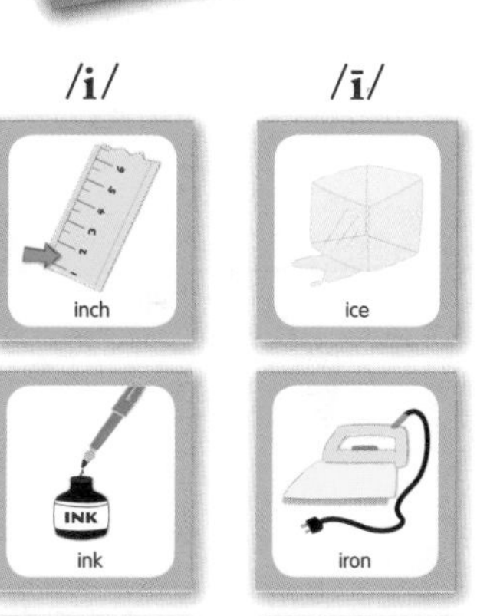

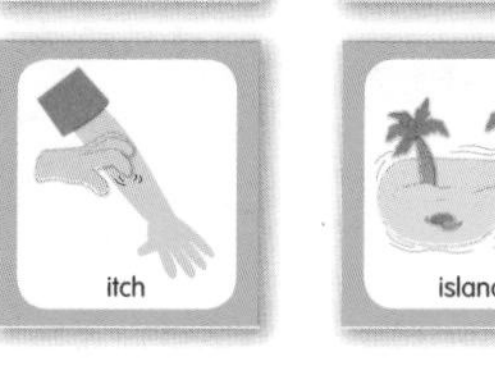

4. Short Ii as an Initial Sound
Point to the words on the puppet as you say, *Sometimes, the letter **Ii** makes the /i/ sound heard in **Izzy** and **iguana**.* Emphasize the beginning sound when you say the words. Then run your finger under the name **Izzy**, emphasizing the pronunciation of each letter. Now read the word **iguana** the same way. After reading each word, ask students, *Where do you hear the /i/ sound?*

Use the picture cards to identify other words that begin with the /i/ sound. Recite the chant on the back of each card as you show the card to the students. Say the word and have them echo you.

Place the three cards that show /i/ (short **i**) words in the puppet's front pocket. Save the three cards with the /ī/ (long **i**) words to introduce later. *(See page 218.)*

5. Review
Help students make their take-home mini-puppets. Then teach students the chant on the back of the mini-puppet and guide them through the activities to review the name, formation, and sound of **Ii**.

I am Izzy.

I am an iguana.

fold

Trace and write the letters.

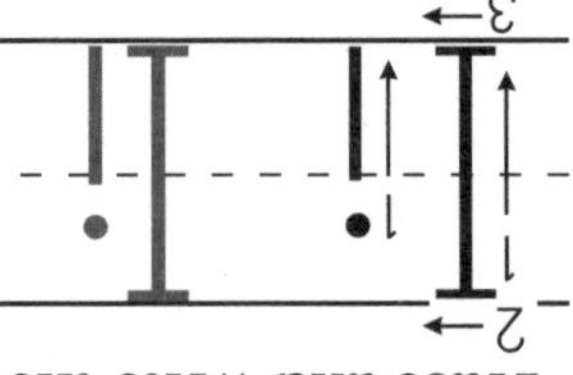

I am Izzy, the iguana.
Say my name.
What other words start the same?

Color the ones that begin with the short **i** sound.

INK

Note: Cut along dashed lines. Glue figure to front of construction paper mitt, above the pocket. *(See page 7 for mitt template and instructions.)*

Note: Cut along dashed lines. Glue name strip across front pocket of construction paper mitt. Glue rhyme and alphabet chart to back of mitt, above the pocket. *(See page 7 for mitt template and instructions.)*

Ii

Izzy, the iguana

I am Izzy, the iguana.
Let's play a game.
Listen to the /i/ sound in my name.

Aa	Bb	Cc	Dd	Ee	Ff	Gg
Hh	Ii	Jj	Kk	Ll	Mm	Nn
Oo	Pp	Qq	Rr	Ss	Tt	Uu
Vv	Ww	Xx	Yy	Zz		

Izzy, the iguana

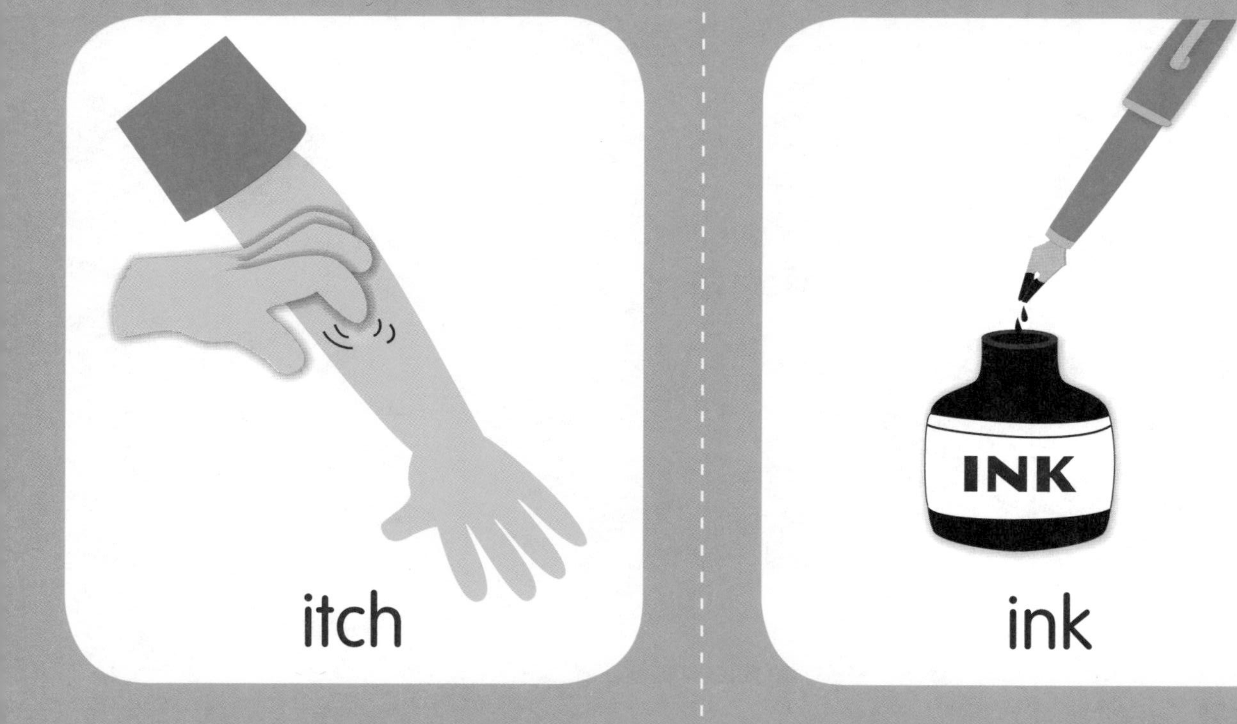

itch

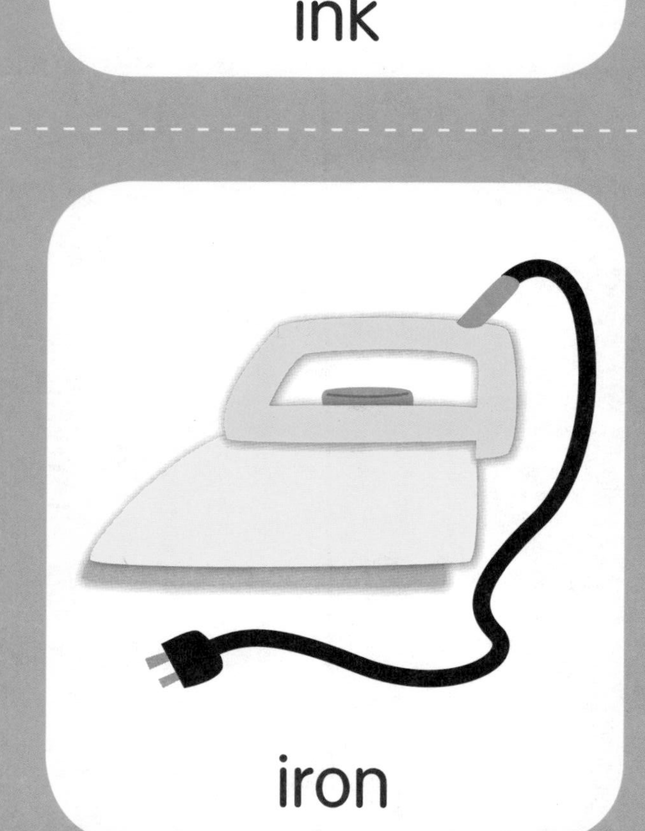

ink

inch

island

iron

ice

Look at Izzy, the iguana.
Think of his name.
What other word
starts the same?

Look at Izzy, the iguana.
Think of his name.
What other word
starts the same?

Look at Izzy, the iguana.
Think of his name.
What other word
starts the same?

Look at Ivy, the iguana.
Think of her name.
What other word
starts the same?

Look at Ivy, the iguana.
Think of her name.
What other word
starts the same?

Look at Ivy, the iguana.
Think of her name.
What other word
starts the same?

Jj Let's meet Jackie, the jaguar

1. **See and Say Jj**
   Introduce the puppet. Say, *Let's meet Jackie, the jaguar.* Point to the letters on the puppet and say that every letter of the alphabet has two forms: big (capital) and little (lowercase). Recite the chant on the back of the puppet and help students practice the /j/ sound.

2. **How to Write Jj**
   Trace the letters on the puppet with your finger to show the correct way to form capital **J** and lowercase **j**. Have students use their fingers in the air to form the letters with you. Verbalize the movements as you go. Say, for example, *Capital J starts at the top and goes down, then curves around at the bottom and up,* etc.

3. **Jj's Place in the Alphabet**
   Use the back of the puppet to show **Jj**'s relative position in the alphabet. Have students sing the alphabet song and clap when they say **Jj**.

4. **Jj as an Initial Sound**
   Point to the words on the puppet as you say, *The letter **Jj** makes the /j/ sound heard in **Jackie** and **jaguar**.* Emphasize the beginning sound when you say the words. Then run your finger under the name **Jackie**, emphasizing the pronunciation of each letter. Now read the word **jaguar** the same way. After reading each word, ask students, *Where do you hear the /j/ sound?*

   Use the picture cards to identify other words that begin with the /j/ sound. Recite the chant on the back of each card as you show the card to the students. Say the word and have them echo you.

   After you identify the initial /j/ sound for each card, place the card in the puppet's front pocket.

5. **Review**
   Help students make their take-home mini-puppets. Then teach students the chant on the back of the mini-puppet and guide them through the activities to review the name, formation, and sound of **Jj**.

Trace and write the letters.

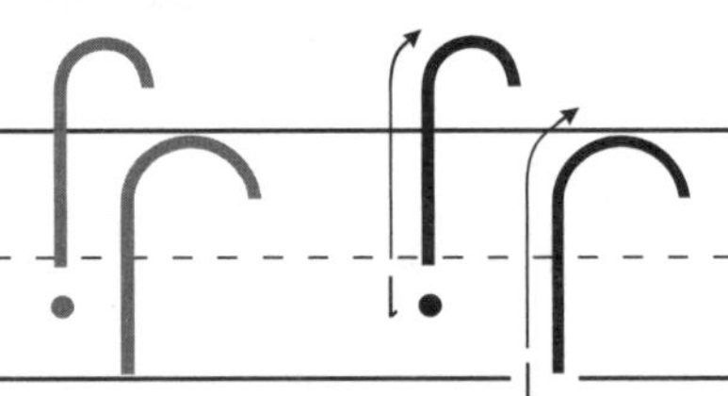

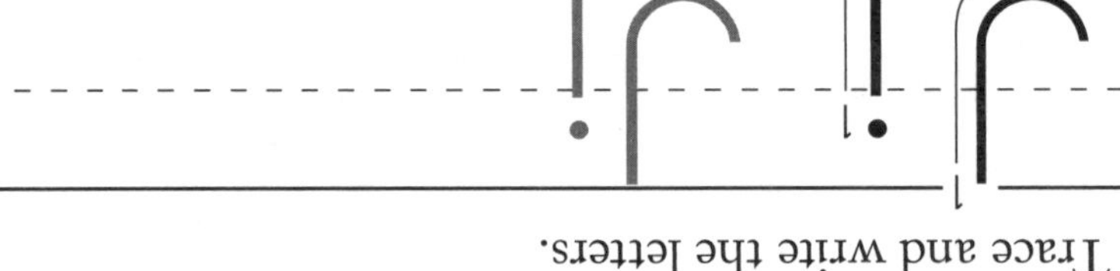

I am Jackie, the jaguar.
Say my name.
What other words start the same?

Color the ones that begin with /j/.

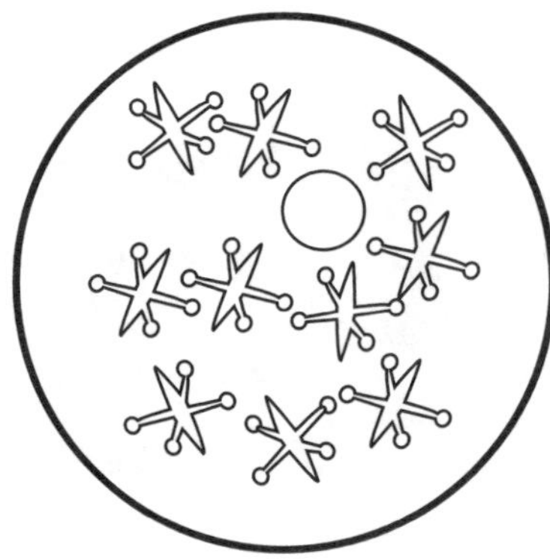

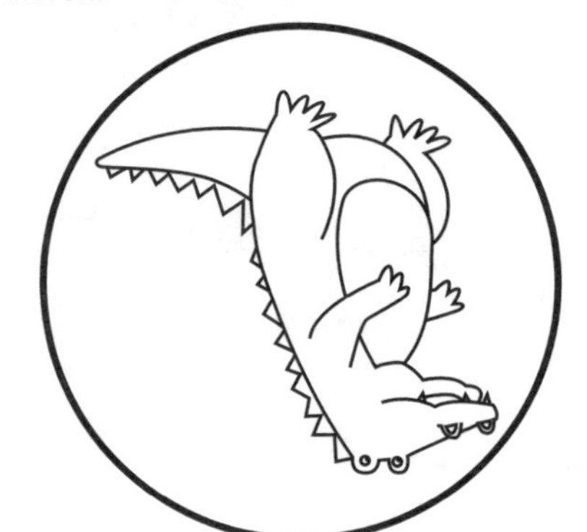

fold

I am Jackie.

I am a jaguar.

Note: Cut along dashed lines. Glue figure to front of construction paper mitt, above the pocket. *(See page 7 for mitt template and instructions.)*

Note: Cut along dashed lines. Glue name strip across front pocket of construction paper mitt. Glue rhyme and alphabet chart to back of mitt, above the pocket. *(See page 7 for mitt template and instructions.)*

Jackie, the Jaguar

I am Jackie, the jaguar.
Let's play a game.
Listen to the /j/ sound in my name.

Aa	Bb	Cc	Dd	Ee	Ff	Gg
Hh	Ii	Jj	Kk	Ll	Mm	Nn
Oo	Pp	Qq	Rr	Ss	Tt	Uu
Vv	Ww	Xx	Yy	Zz		

Jackie, the jaguar

jar

jam

jacks

jet

jellyfish

jeep

Look at Jackie, the jaguar.
Think of her name.
What other word
starts the same?

Look at Jackie, the jaguar.
Think of her name.
What other word
starts the same?

Look at Jackie, the jaguar.
Think of her name.
What other word
starts the same?

Look at Jackie, the jaguar.
Think of her name.
What other word
starts the same?

Look at Jackie, the jaguar.
Think of her name.
What other word
starts the same?

Look at Jackie, the jaguar.
Think of her name.
What other word
starts the same?

Let's meet

Kim, the koala

1. See and Say Kk

Introduce the puppet. Say, *Let's meet Kim, the koala.* Point to the letters on the puppet and say that every letter of the alphabet has two forms: big (capital) and little (lowercase). Recite the chant on the back of the puppet and help students practice the /k/ sound.

2. How to Write Kk

Trace the letters on the puppet with your finger to show the correct way to form capital **K** and lowercase **k**. Have students use their fingers in the air to form the letters with you. Verbalize the movements as you go. Say, for example, *Capital **K** starts at the top, make a straight stick down, go back to the top and make a slanted stick to the middle,* etc.

3. Kk's Place in the Alphabet

Use the back of the puppet to show **Kk**'s relative position in the alphabet. Have students sing the alphabet song and clap when they say **Kk**.

4. Kk as an Initial Sound

Point to the words on the puppet as you say, *The letter **Kk** makes the /k/ sound heard in **Kim** and **koala**.* Emphasize the beginning sound when you say the words. Then run your finger under the name **Kim**, emphasizing the pronunciation of each letter. Now read the word **koala** the same way. After reading each word, ask students, *Where do you hear the /k/ sound?*

Use the picture cards to identify other words that begin with the /k/ sound. Recite the chant on the back of each card as you show the card to the students. Say the word and have them echo you.

After you identify the initial /k/ sound for each card, place the card in the puppet's front pocket.

5. Review

Help students make their take-home mini-puppets. Then teach students the chant on the back of the mini-puppet and guide them through the activities to review the name, formation, and sound of **Kk**.

I am Kim.

I am a koala.

Trace and write the letters.

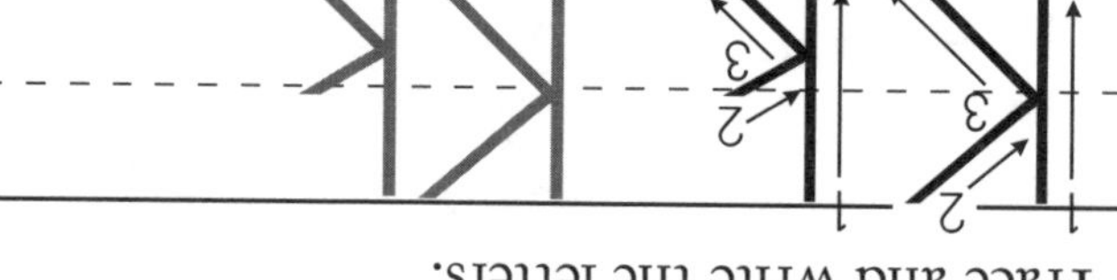

I am Kim, the koala.
Say my name.
What other words start the same?

Color the ones that begin with /k/.

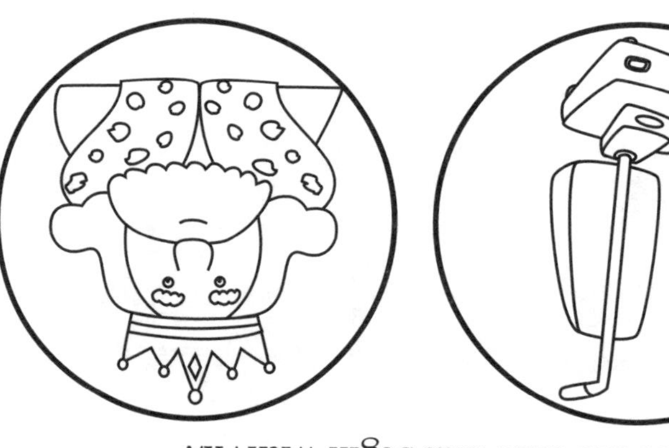

Note: Cut along dashed lines. Glue figure to front of construction paper mitt, above the pocket. *(See page 7 for mitt template and instructions.)*

Note: Cut along dashed lines. Glue name strip across front pocket of construction paper mitt. Glue rhyme and alphabet chart to back of mitt, above the pocket. *(See page 7 for mitt template and instructions.)*

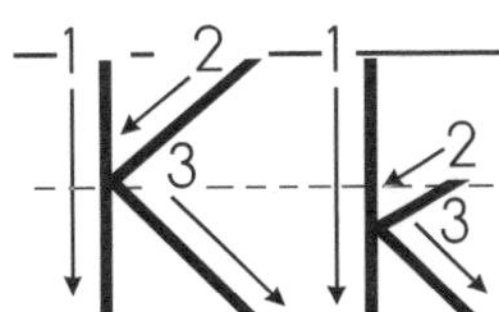

Kim, the koala

I am Kim, the koala.
Let's play a game.
Listen to the /k/ sound in my name.

Aa	Bb	Cc	Dd	Ee	Ff	Gg
Hh	Ii	Jj	Kk	Ll	Mm	Nn
Oo	Pp	Qq	Rr	Ss	Tt	Uu
Vv	Ww	Xx	Yy	Zz		

Kim, the koala

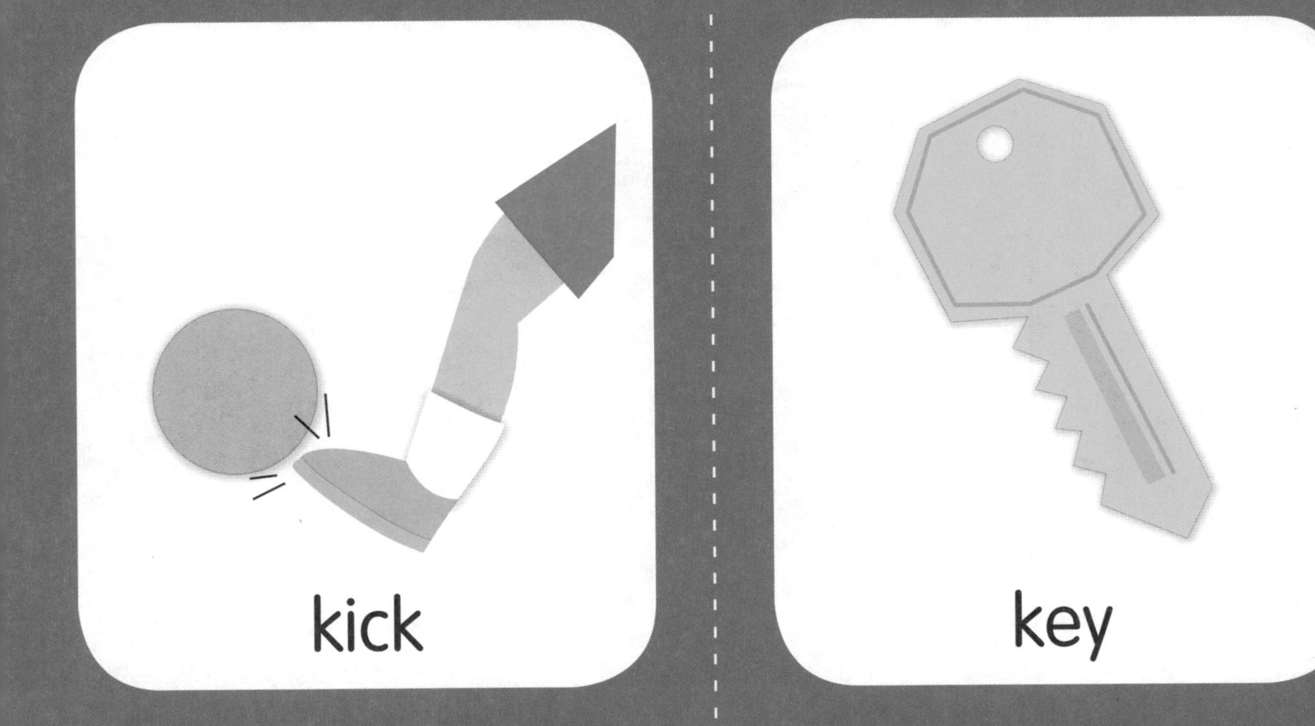

kick

key

kangaroo

kitten

kite

king

Look at Kim, the koala.
Think of her name.
What other word
starts the same?

Look at Kim, the koala.
Think of her name.
What other word
starts the same?

© Evan-Moor Corp. • EMC 2005

Look at Kim, the koala.
Think of her name.
What other word
starts the same?

© Evan-Moor Corp. • EMC 2005

Look at Kim, the koala.
Think of her name.
What other word
starts the same?

© Evan-Moor Corp. • EMC 2005

Look at Kim, the koala.
Think of her name.
What other word
starts the same?

© Evan-Moor Corp. • EMC 2005

Look at Kim, the koala.
Think of her name.
What other word
starts the same?

© Evan-Moor Corp. • EMC 2005

Ll Let's meet Lucy, the lamb

1. **See and Say Ll**
   Introduce the puppet. Say, *Let's meet Lucy, the lamb.* Point to the letters on the puppet and say that every letter of the alphabet has two forms: big (capital) and little (lowercase). Recite the chant on the back of the puppet and help students practice the /l/ sound.

2. **How to Write Ll**
   Trace the letters on the puppet with your finger to show the correct way to form capital **L** and lowercase **l**. Have students use their fingers in the air to form the letters with you. Verbalize the movements as you go. Say, for example, *Capital* ***L*** *starts at the top, make a long stick down, and add a line across the bottom,* etc.

3. **Ll's Place in the Alphabet**
   Use the back of the puppet to show **Ll**'s relative position in the alphabet. Have students sing the alphabet song and clap when they say **Ll**.

4. **Ll as an Initial Sound**
   Point to the words on the puppet as you say, *The letter* ***Ll*** *makes the /l/ sound heard in* ***Lucy*** *and* ***lamb***. Emphasize the beginning sound when you say the words. Then run your finger under the name **Lucy**, emphasizing the pronunciation of each letter. Now read the word **lamb** the same way. After reading each word, ask students, *Where do you hear the /l/ sound?*

   Use the picture cards to identify other words that begin with the /l/ sound. Recite the chant on the back of each card as you show the card to the students. Say the word and have them echo you.

   After you identify the initial /l/ sound for each card, place the card in the puppet's front pocket.

5. **Review**
   Help students make their take-home mini-puppets. Then teach students the chant on the back of the mini-puppet and guide them through the activities to review the name, formation, and sound of **Ll**.

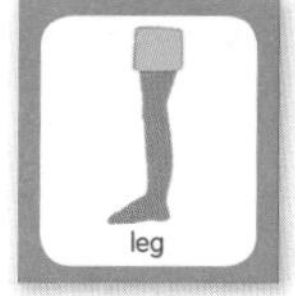

Trace and write the letters.

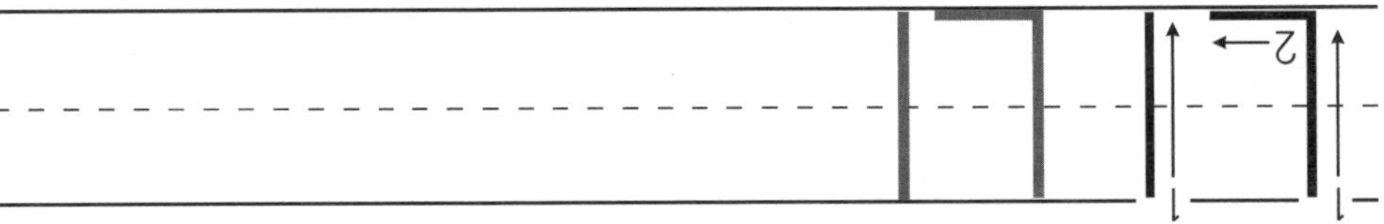

I am Lucy, the lamb.
Say my name.
What other words start the same?

Color the ones that begin with /l/.

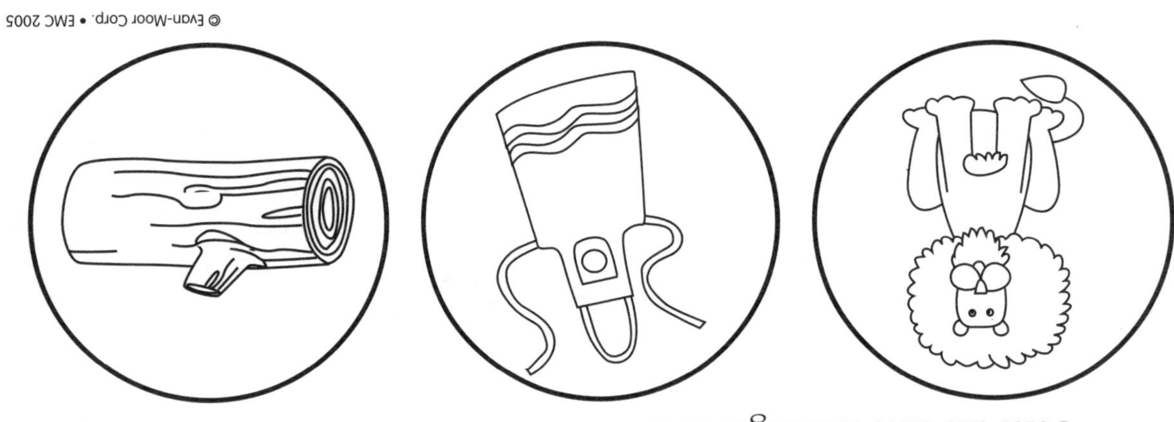

fold

I am Lucy.

I am a lamb.

Note: Cut along dashed lines. Glue figure to front of construction paper mitt, above the pocket. *(See page 7 for mitt template and instructions.)*

Note: Cut along dashed lines. Glue name strip across front pocket of construction paper mitt. Glue rhyme and alphabet chart to back of mitt, above the pocket. *(See page 7 for mitt template and instructions.)*

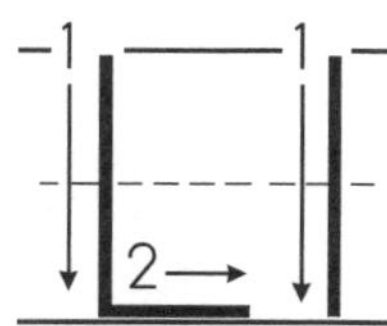

Lucy, the lamb

I am Lucy, the lamb.
Let's play a game.
Listen to the /l/ sound in my name.

Aa	Bb	Cc	Dd	Ee	Ff	Gg
Hh	Ii	Jj	Kk	Ll	Mm	Nn
Oo	Pp	Qq	Rr	Ss	Tt	Uu
Vv	Ww	Xx	Yy	Zz		

Lucy, the lamb

leg
leaf
ladder
lamp
log
lion

Look at Lucy, the lamb.
Think of her name.
What other word
starts the same?

Ll

Look at Lucy, the lamb.
Think of her name.
What other word
starts the same?

© Evan-Moor Corp. • EMC 2005

Ll

Look at Lucy, the lamb.
Think of her name.
What other word
starts the same?

© Evan-Moor Corp. • EMC 2005

Ll

Look at Lucy, the lamb.
Think of her name.
What other word
starts the same?

© Evan-Moor Corp. • EMC 2005

Ll

Look at Lucy, the lamb.
Think of her name.
What other word
starts the same?

© Evan-Moor Corp. • EMC 2005

Ll

Look at Lucy, the lamb.
Think of her name.
What other word
starts the same?

© Evan-Moor Corp. • EMC 2005

Mm Let's meet Mortie, the mouse

1. See and Say Mm

Introduce the puppet. Say, *Let's meet Mortie, the mouse.* Point to the letters on the puppet and say that every letter of the alphabet has two forms: big (capital) and little (lowercase). Recite the chant on the back of the puppet and help students practice the /m/ sound.

2. How to Write Mm

Trace the letters on the puppet with your finger to show the correct way to form capital **M** and lowercase **m**. Have students use their fingers in the air to form the letters with you. Verbalize the movements as you go. Say, for example, *Capital **M** has four sticks that all start at the top. Make two straight sticks on each side and two slanted sticks in between,* etc.

3. Mm's Place in the Alphabet

Use the back of the puppet to show **Mm**'s relative position in the alphabet. Have students sing the alphabet song and clap when they say **Mm**.

4. Mm as an Initial Sound

Point to the words on the puppet as you say, *The letter **Mm** makes the /m/ sound heard in **Mortie** and **mouse**.* Emphasize the beginning sound when you say the words. Then run your finger under the name **Mortie**, emphasizing the pronunciation of each letter. Now read the word **mouse** the same way. After reading each word, ask students, *Where do you hear the /m/ sound?*

Use the picture cards to identify other words that begin with the /m/ sound. Recite the chant on the back of each card as you show the card to the students. Say the word and have them echo you.

After you identify the initial /m/ sound for each card, place the card in the puppet's front pocket.

5. Review

Help students make their take-home mini-puppets. Then teach students the chant on the back of the mini-puppet and guide them through the activities to review the name, formation, and sound of **Mm**.

Trace and write the letters.

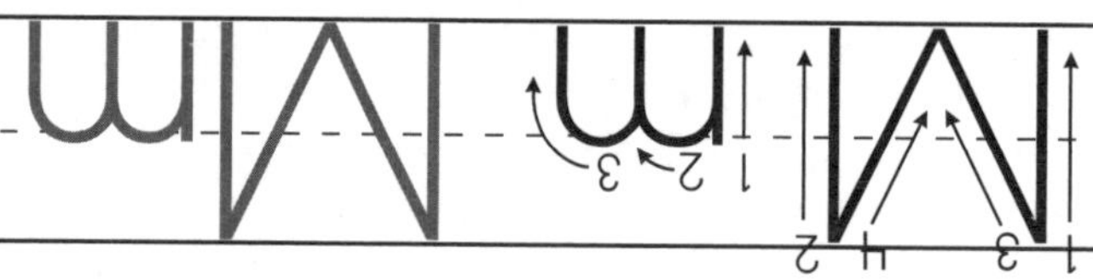

I am Mortie, the mouse.
Say my name.
What other words start the same?

Color the ones that begin with /m/.

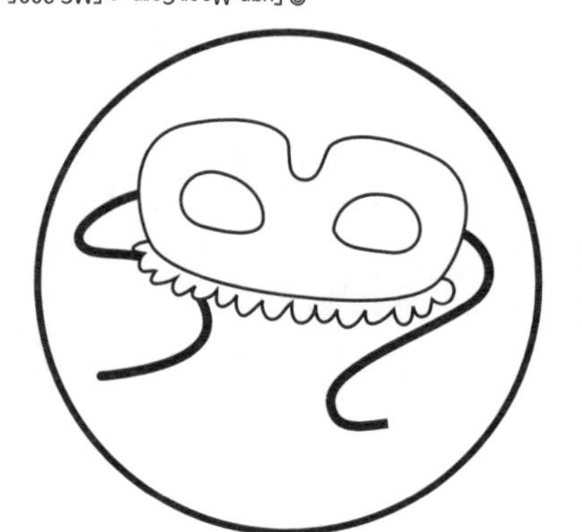

fold

I am Mortie.

I am a mouse.

Note: Cut along dashed lines. Glue figure to front of construction paper mitt, above the pocket.
(See page 7 for mitt template and instructions.)

Note: Cut along dashed lines. Glue name strip across front pocket of construction paper mitt. Glue rhyme and alphabet chart to back of mitt, above the pocket. *(See page 7 for mitt template and instructions.)*

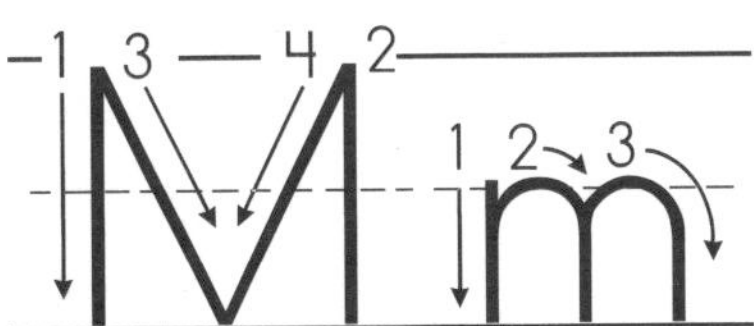

Mortie, the mouse

I am Mortie, the mouse.
Let's play a game.
Listen to the /m/ sound in my name.

Aa	Bb	Cc	Dd	Ee	Ff	Gg
Hh	Ii	Jj	Kk	Ll	Mm	Nn
Oo	Pp	Qq	Rr	Ss	Tt	Uu
Vv	Ww	Xx	Yy	Zz		

Mortie, the mouse

mittens

mask

magnet

mice

mop

monkey

Look at Mortie, the mouse.
Think of his name.
What other word
starts the same?

Look at Mortie, the mouse.
Think of his name.
What other word
starts the same?

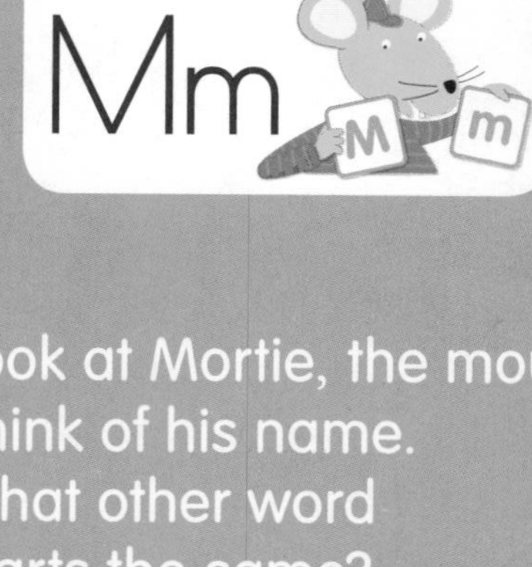

Look at Mortie, the mouse.
Think of his name.
What other word
starts the same?

Look at Mortie, the mouse.
Think of his name.
What other word
starts the same?

Look at Mortie, the mouse.
Think of his name.
What other word
starts the same?

Look at Mortie, the mouse.
Think of his name.
What other word
starts the same?

Nn Let's meet Nancy, the nightingale

1. **See and Say Nn**
   Introduce the puppet. Say, *Let's meet Nancy, the nightingale.* Point to the letters on the puppet and say that every letter of the alphabet has two forms: big (capital) and little (lowercase). Recite the chant on the back of the puppet and help students practice the /n/ sound.

2. **How to Write Nn**
   Trace the letters on the puppet with your finger to show the correct way to form capital **N** and lowercase **n**. Have students use their fingers in the air to form the letters with you. Verbalize the movements as you go. Say, for example, *Capital N has three sticks that all start at the top. Make two straight sticks on each side and a slanted stick in between,* etc.

3. **Nn's Place in the Alphabet**
   Use the back of the puppet to show **Nn**'s relative position in the alphabet. Have students sing the alphabet song and clap when they say **Nn**.

4. **Nn as an Initial Sound**
   Point to the words on the puppet as you say, *The letter **Nn** makes the /n/ sound heard in **Nancy** and **nightingale**.* Emphasize the beginning sound when you say the words. Then run your finger under the name **Nancy**, emphasizing the pronunciation of each letter. Now read the word **nightingale** the same way. After reading each word, ask students, *Where do you hear the /n/ sound?*

   Use the picture cards to identify other words that begin with the /n/ sound. Recite the chant on the back of each card as you show the card to the students. Say the word and have them echo you.

   After you identify the initial /n/ sound for each card, place the card in the puppet's front pocket.

5. **Review**
   Help students make their take-home mini-puppets. Then teach students the chant on the back of the mini-puppet and guide them through the activities to review the name, formation, and sound of **Nn**.

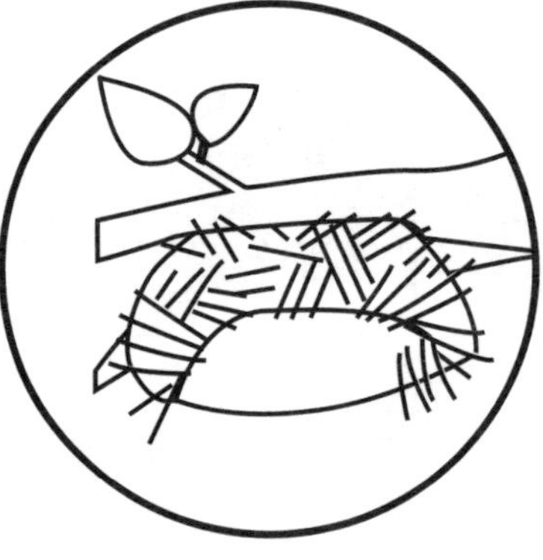

Color the ones that begin with /n/.

I am Nancy, the nightingale.
Say my name.
What other words start the same?

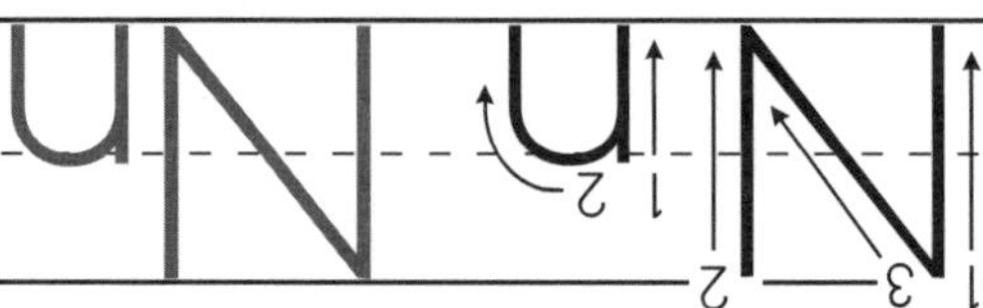

Trace and write the letters.

fold

I am Nancy.

I am a nightingale.

Note: Cut along dashed lines. Glue figure to front of construction paper mitt, above the pocket. *(See page 7 for mitt template and instructions.)*

Note: Cut along dashed lines. Glue name strip across front pocket of construction paper mitt. Glue rhyme and alphabet chart to back of mitt, above the pocket. *(See page 7 for mitt template and instructions.)*

Nn

Nancy, the nightingale

I am Nancy, the nightingale.
Let's play a game.
Listen to the /n/ sound in my name.

Aa	Bb	Cc	Dd	Ee	Ff	Gg
Hh	Ii	Jj	Kk	Ll	Mm	Nn
Oo	Pp	Qq	Rr	Ss	Tt	Uu
Vv	Ww	Xx	Yy	Zz		

Nancy, the nightingale

nickel

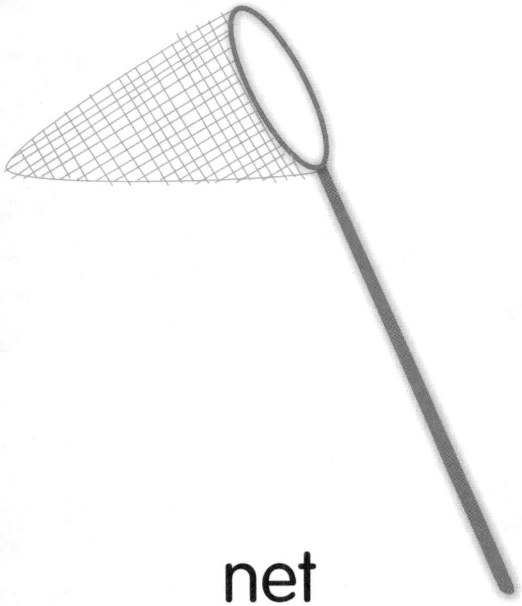

net

nest

nuts

nose

nine

Look at Nancy,
the nightingale.
Think of her name.
What other word
starts the same?

Look at Nancy,
the nightingale.
Think of her name.
What other word
starts the same?

© Evan-Moor Corp. • EMC 2005

Look at Nancy,
the nightingale.
Think of her name.
What other word
starts the same?

© Evan-Moor Corp. • EMC 2005

Look at Nancy,
the nightingale.
Think of her name.
What other word
starts the same?

© Evan-Moor Corp. • EMC 2005

Look at Nancy,
the nightingale.
Think of her name.
What other word
starts the same?

© Evan-Moor Corp. • EMC 2005

Look at Nancy,
the nightingale.
Think of her name.
What other word
starts the same?

© Evan-Moor Corp. • EMC 2005

Oo Let's meet Ollie, the otter

1. See and Say Oo

Introduce the puppet. Say, *Let's meet Ollie, the otter.* Point to the letters on the puppet and say that every letter of the alphabet has two forms: big (capital) and little (lowercase). Recite the chant on the back of the puppet and help students practice the short **o** sound.

2. How to Write Oo

Trace the letters on the puppet with your finger to show the correct way to form capital **O** and lowercase **o**. Have students use their fingers in the air to form the letters with you. Verbalize the movements as you go. Say, for example, *Capital **O** begins near the top, goes over the hill and around,* etc.

/o/ /ō/

3. Oo's Place in the Alphabet

Use the back of the puppet to show **Oo**'s relative position in the alphabet. Have students sing the alphabet song and clap when they say **Oo**.

4. Short Oo as an Initial Sound

Point to the words on the puppet as you say, *Sometimes, the letter **Oo** makes the /o/ sound heard in **Ollie** and **otter**.* Emphasize the beginning sound when you say the words. Then run your finger under the name **Ollie**, emphasizing the pronunciation of each letter. Now read the word **otter** the same way. After reading each word, ask students, *Where do you hear the /o/ sound?*

Use the picture cards to identify other words that begin with the /o/ sound. Recite the chant on the back of each card as you show the card to the students. Say the word and have them echo you.

Place the three cards that show /o/ (short **o**) words in the puppet's front pocket. Save the three cards with /ō/ (long **o**) words to introduce later. *(See page 218.)*

5. Review

Help students make their take-home mini-puppets. Then teach students the chant on the back of the mini-puppet and guide them through the activities to review the name, formation, and sound of **Oo**.

fold

I am Ollie.

I am an otter.

Trace and write the letters.

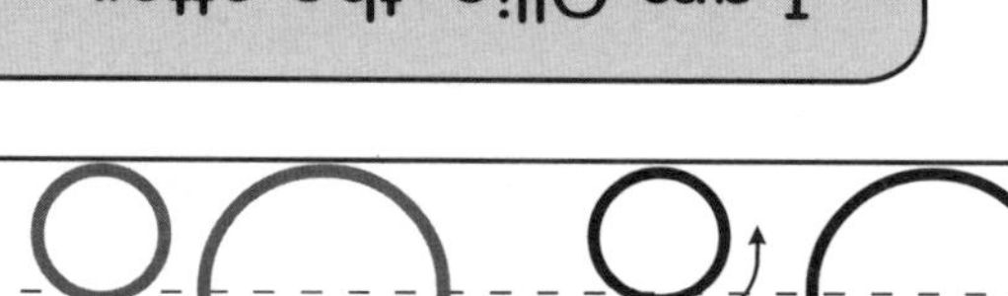

I am Ollie, the otter.
Say my name.
What other words start the same?

Color the ones that begin with the short **o** sound.

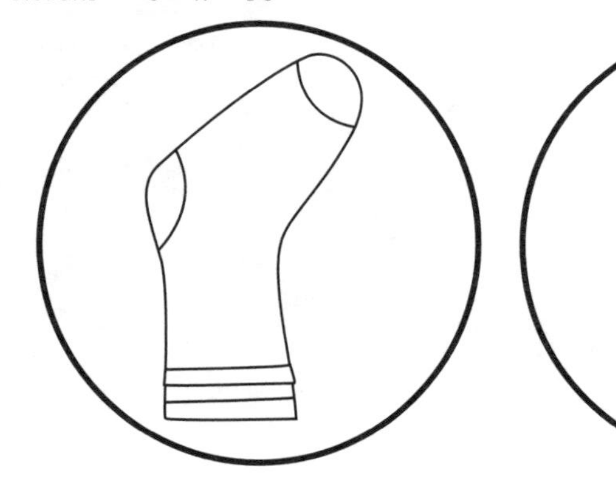

Note: Cut along dashed lines. Glue figure to front of construction paper mitt, above the pocket.
(See page 7 for mitt template and instructions.)

Note: Cut along dashed lines. Glue name strip across front pocket of construction paper mitt. Glue rhyme and alphabet chart to back of mitt, above the pocket. *(See page 7 for mitt template and instructions.)*

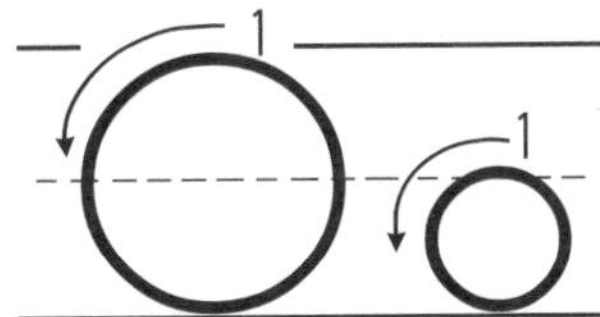

Ollie, the otter

I am Ollie, the otter.
Let's play a game.
Listen to the /o/ sound in my name.

Aa Bb Cc Dd Ee Ff Gg
Hh Ii Jj Kk Ll Mm Nn
Oo Pp Qq Rr Ss Tt Uu
Vv Ww Xx Yy Zz

Ollie, the otter

octopus

ostrich

off on

overalls

oboe

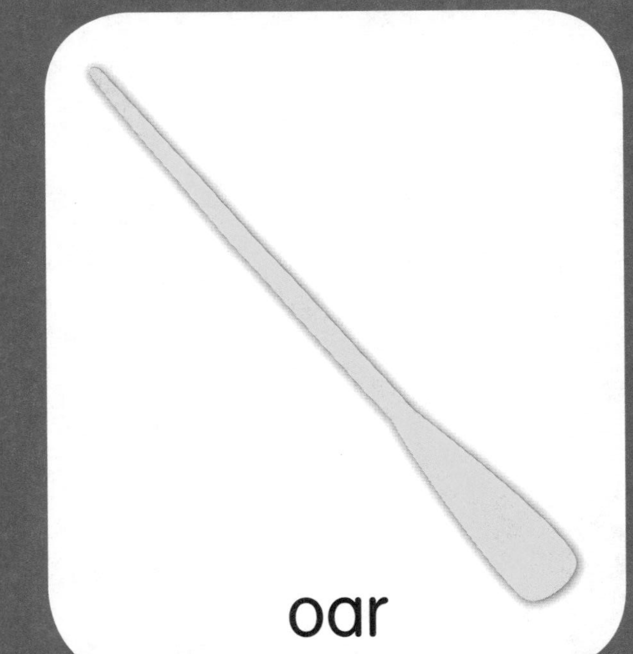

oar

Look at Ollie, the otter.
Think of his name.
What other word
starts the same?

Look at Ollie, the otter.
Think of his name.
What other word
starts the same?

Look at Ollie, the otter.
Think of his name.
What other word
starts the same?

Look at Oki, the otter.
Think of her name.
What other word
starts the same?

Look at Oki, the otter.
Think of her name.
What other word
starts the same?

Look at Oki, the otter.
Think of her name.
What other word
starts the same?

Pp Let's meet Pinky, the pig

1. See and Say Pp

Introduce the puppet. Say, *Let's meet Pinky, the pig.* Point to the letters on the puppet and say that every letter of the alphabet has two forms: big (capital) and little (lowercase). Recite the chant on the back of the puppet and help students practice the /p/ sound.

2. How to Write Pp

Trace the letters on the puppet with your finger to show the correct way to form capital **P** and lowercase **p**. Have students use their fingers in the air to form the letters with you. Verbalize the movements as you go. Say, for example, *Capital **P** starts at the top, make a long stick down, and then go back to the top and curve around,* etc.

3. Pp's Place in the Alphabet

Use the back of the puppet to show **Pp**'s relative position in the alphabet. Have students sing the alphabet song and clap when they say **Pp**.

4. Pp as an Initial Sound

Point to the words on the puppet as you say, *The letter **Pp** makes the /p/ sound heard in **Pinky** and **pig**.* Emphasize the beginning sound when you say the words. Then run your finger under the name **Pinky**, emphasizing the pronunciation of each letter. Now read the word **pig** the same way. After reading each word, ask students, *Where do you hear the /p/ sound?*

Use the picture cards to identify other words that begin with the /p/ sound. Recite the chant on the back of each card as you show the card to the students. Say the word and have them echo you.

After you identify the initial /p/ sound for each card, place the card in the puppet's front pocket.

5. Review

Help students make their take-home mini-puppets. Then teach students the chant on the back of the mini-puppet and guide them through the activities to review the name, formation, and sound of **Pp**.

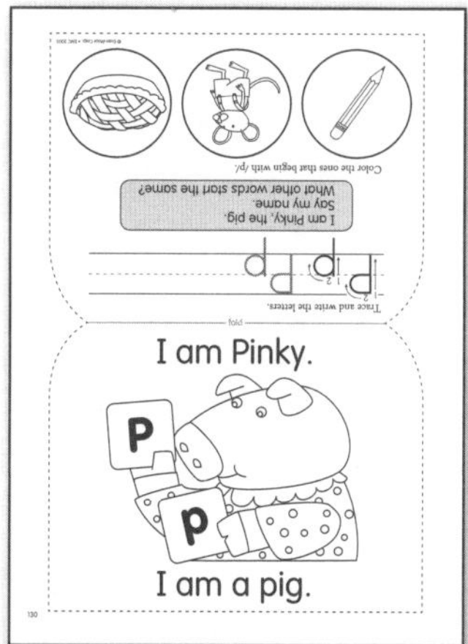

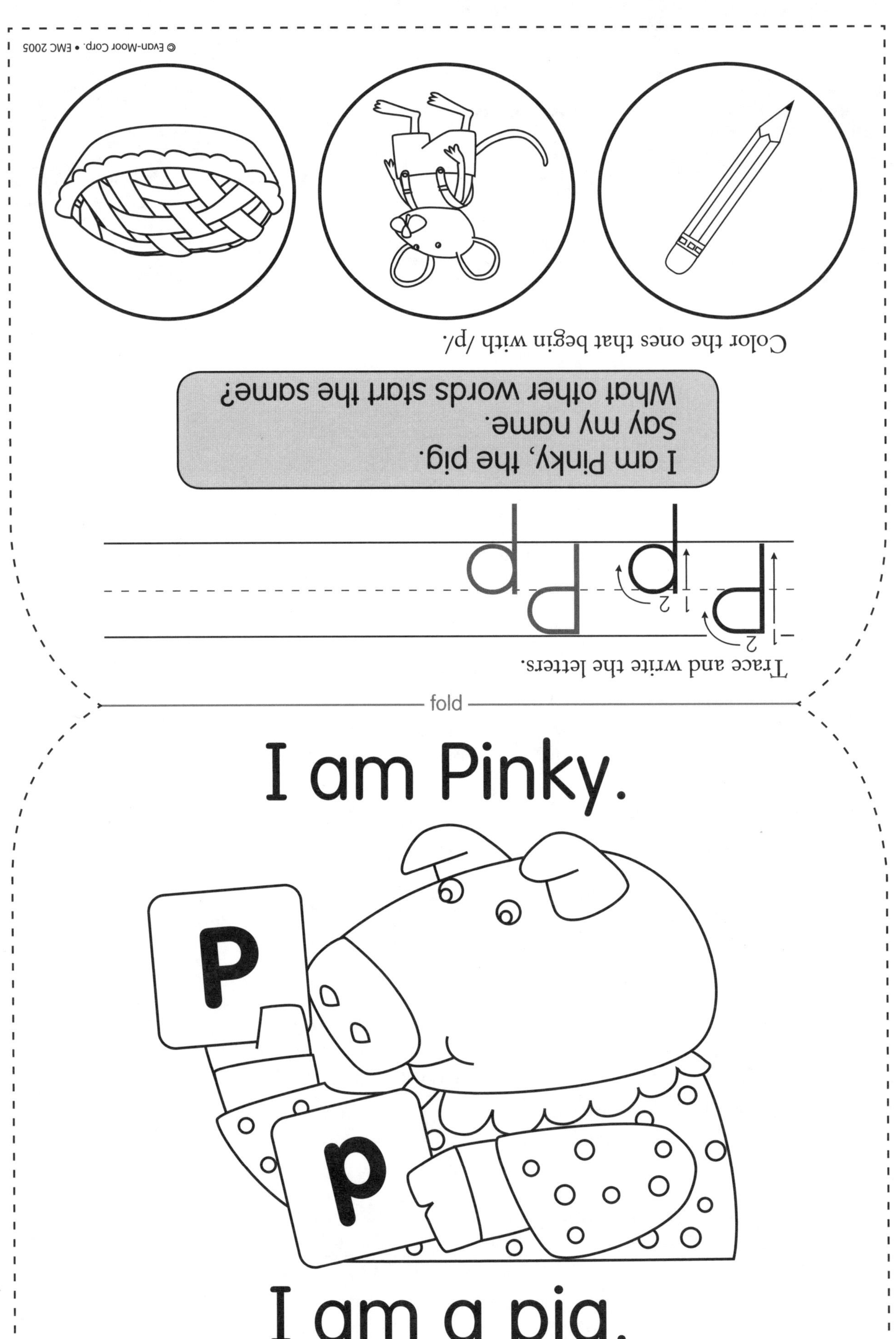
© Evan-Moor Corp. • EMC 2005
Color the ones that begin with /p/.
I am Pinky, the pig.
Say my name.
What other words start the same?
Trace and write the letters.
Pp
fold
I am Pinky.
P
p
I am a pig.

Note: Cut along dashed lines. Glue figure to front of construction paper mitt, above the pocket. *(See page 7 for mitt template and instructions.)*

Note: Cut along dashed lines. Glue name strip across front pocket of construction paper mitt. Glue rhyme and alphabet chart to back of mitt, above the pocket. *(See page 7 for mitt template and instructions.)*

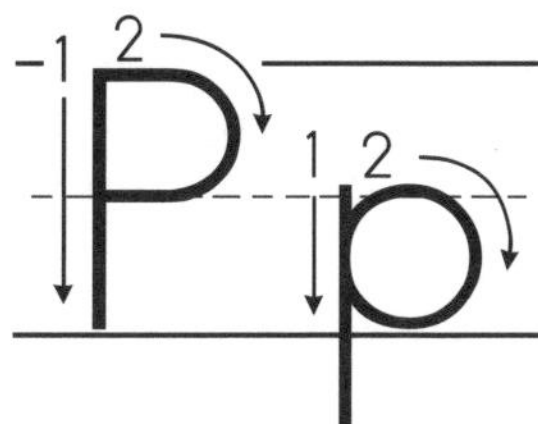

Pinky, the pig

I am Pinky, the pig.
Let's play a game.
Listen to the /p/ sound in my name.

Aa	Bb	Cc	Dd	Ee	Ff	Gg
Hh	Ii	Jj	Kk	Ll	Mm	Nn
Oo	Pp	Qq	Rr	Ss	Tt	Uu
Vv	Ww	Xx	Yy	Zz		

Pinky, the pig

pencil
panda
paint
pumpkin
pot
pie

Look at Pinky, the pig.
Think of her name.
What other word
starts the same?

Look at Pinky, the pig.
Think of her name.
What other word
starts the same?

Look at Pinky, the pig.
Think of her name.
What other word
starts the same?

Look at Pinky, the pig.
Think of her name.
What other word
starts the same?

Look at Pinky, the pig.
Think of her name.
What other word
starts the same?

Look at Pinky, the pig.
Think of her name.
What other word
starts the same?

Qq Let's meet Quincy, the quail

1. See and Say Qq

Introduce the puppet. Say, *Let's meet Quincy, the quail.* Point to the letters on the puppet and say that every letter of the alphabet has two forms: big (capital) and little (lowercase). Recite the chant on the back of the puppet and help students practice the /kw/ sound.

2. How to Write Qq

Trace the letters on the puppet with your finger to show the correct way to form capital **Q** and lowercase **q**. Have students use their fingers in the air to form the letters with you. Verbalize the movements as you go. Say, for example, *Capital Q begins near the top, curves around to make a circle, and then add a tail,* etc.

3. Qq's Place in the Alphabet

Use the back of the puppet to show **Qq**'s relative position in the alphabet. Have students sing the alphabet song and clap when they say **Qq**.

4. Qq as an Initial Sound

Point to the words on the puppet as you say, *The letter **Qq** makes the /kw/ sound heard in **Quincy** and **quail**.* Emphasize the beginning sound when you say the words. Then run your finger under the name **Quincy**, emphasizing the pronunciation of each letter. Now read the word **quail** the same way. After reading each word, ask students, *Where do you hear the /kw/ sound?*

Use the picture cards to identify other words that begin with the /kw/ sound. Recite the chant on the back of each card as you show the card to the students. Say the word and have them echo you.

After you identify the initial /kw/ sound for each card, place the card in the puppet's front pocket.

5. Review

Help students make their take-home mini-puppets. Then teach students the chant on the back of the mini-puppet and guide them through the activities to review the name, formation, and sound of **Qq**.

Trace and write the letters.

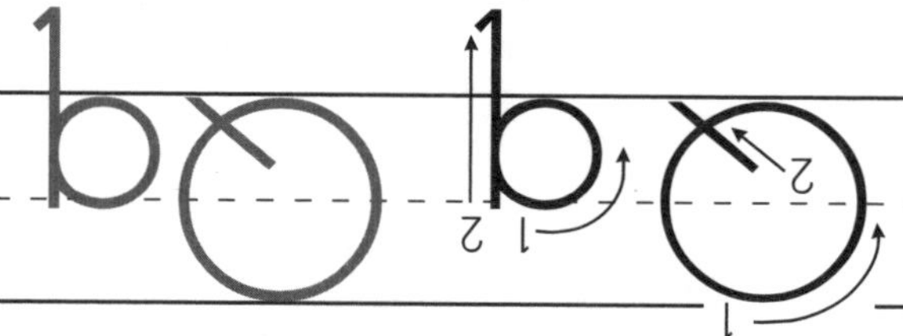

I am Quincy, the quail.
Say my name.
What other words start the same?

Color the ones that begin with /kw/.

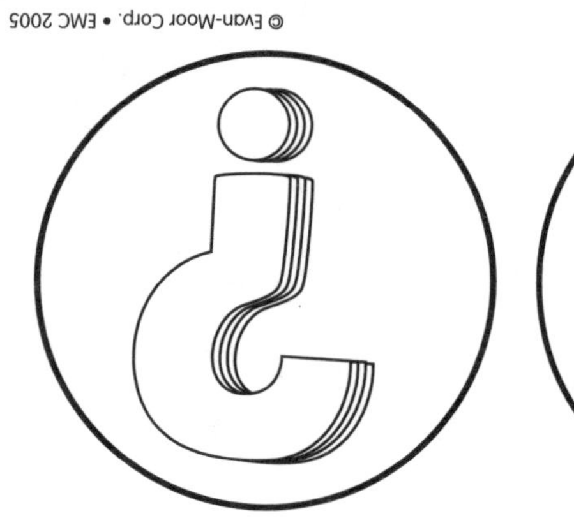

fold

I am Quincy.

I am a quail.

Note: Cut along dashed lines. Glue figure to front of construction paper mitt, above the pocket. *(See page 7 for mitt template and instructions.)*

b

q

Note: Cut along dashed lines. Glue name strip across front pocket of construction paper mitt. Glue rhyme and alphabet chart to back of mitt, above the pocket. *(See page 7 for mitt template and instructions.)*

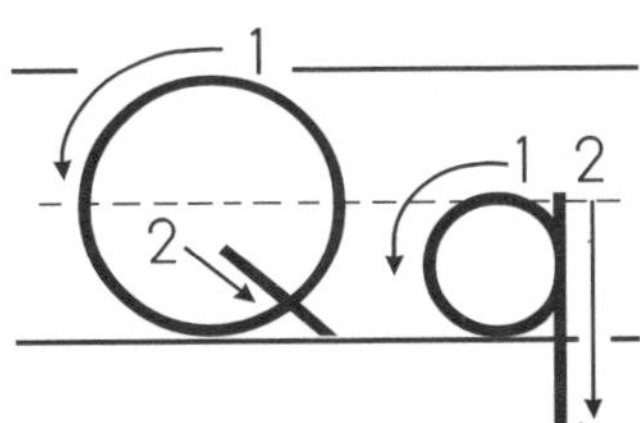

Quincy, the quail

I am Quincy, the quail.
Let's play a game.
Listen to the /kw/ sound in my name.

Aa	Bb	Cc	Dd	Ee	Ff	Gg
Hh	Ii	Jj	Kk	Ll	Mm	Nn
Oo	Pp	Qq	Rr	Ss	Tt	Uu
Vv	Ww	Xx	Yy	Zz		

Quincy, the quail

quarter

quart

quack

quilt

question mark

queen

Look at Quincy, the quail.
Think of his name.
What other word
starts the same?

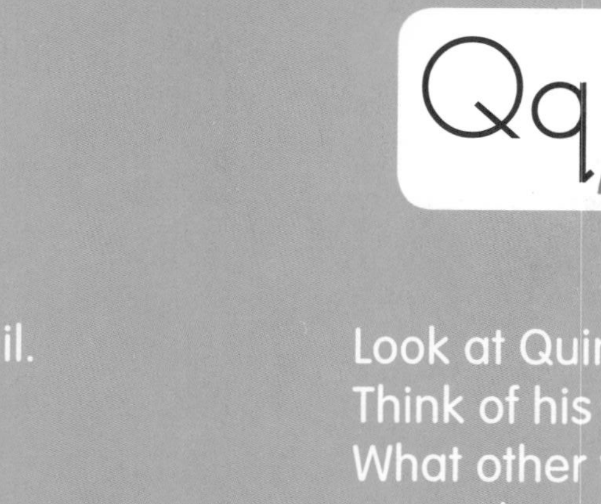

Look at Quincy, the quail.
Think of his name.
What other word
starts the same?

© Evan-Moor Corp. • EMC 2005

Look at Quincy, the quail.
Think of his name.
What other word
starts the same?

© Evan-Moor Corp. • EMC 2005

Look at Quincy, the quail.
Think of his name.
What other word
starts the same?

© Evan-Moor Corp. • EMC 2005

Look at Quincy, the quail.
Think of his name.
What other word
starts the same?

© Evan-Moor Corp. • EMC 2005

Look at Quincy, the quail.
Think of his name.
What other word
starts the same?

© Evan-Moor Corp. • EMC 2005

1. See and Say Rr

Introduce the puppet. Say, *Let's meet Rosie, the rabbit.* Point to the letters on the puppet and say that every letter of the alphabet has two forms: big (capital) and little (lowercase). Recite the chant on the back of the puppet and help students practice the /r/ sound.

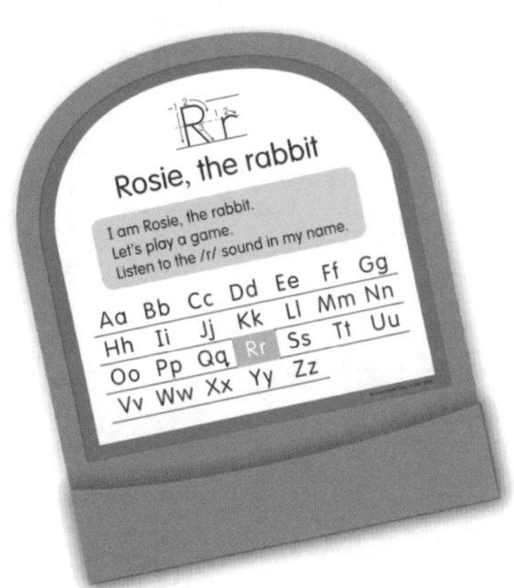

2. How to Write Rr

Trace the letters on the puppet with your finger to show the correct way to form capital **R** and lowercase **r**. Have students use their fingers in the air to form the letters with you. Verbalize the movements as you go. Say, for example, *Capital **R** starts at the top, make a long stick down, then back to the top and curve around,* etc.

3. Rr's Place in the Alphabet

Use the back of the puppet to show **Rr**'s relative position in the alphabet. Have students sing the alphabet song and clap when they say **Rr**.

4. Rr as an Initial Sound

Point to the words on the puppet as you say, *The letter **Rr** makes the /r/ sound heard in **Rosie** and **rabbit**.* Emphasize the beginning sound when you say the words. Then run your finger under the name **Rosie**, emphasizing the pronunciation of each letter. Now read the word **rabbit** the same way. After reading each word, ask students, *Where do you hear the /r/ sound?*

Use the picture cards to identify other words that begin with the /r/ sound. Recite the chant on the back of each card as you show the card to the students. Say the word and have them echo you.

After you identify the initial /r/ sound for each card, place the card in the puppet's front pocket.

5. Review

Help students make their take-home mini-puppets. Then teach students the chant on the back of the mini-puppet and guide them through the activities to review the name, formation, and sound of **Rr**.

Trace and write the letters.

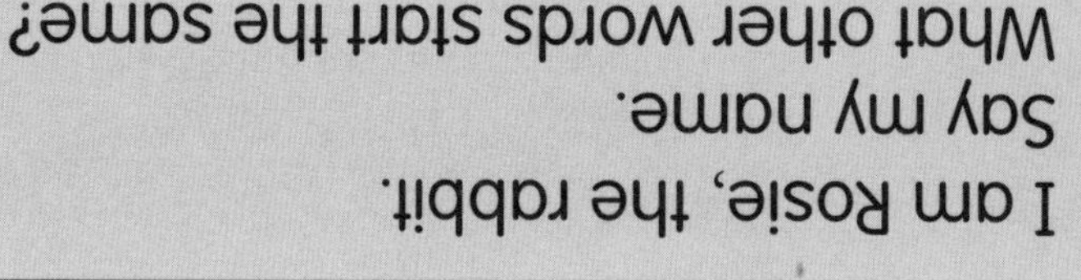

I am Rosie, the rabbit.
Say my name.
What other words start the same?

Color the ones that begin with /r/.

fold

I am Rosie.

I am a rabbit.

Note: Cut along dashed lines. Glue figure to front of construction paper mitt, above the pocket. *(See page 7 for mitt template and instructions.)*

Note: Cut along dashed lines. Glue name strip across front pocket of construction paper mitt. Glue rhyme and alphabet chart to back of mitt, above the pocket. *(See page 7 for mitt template and instructions.)*

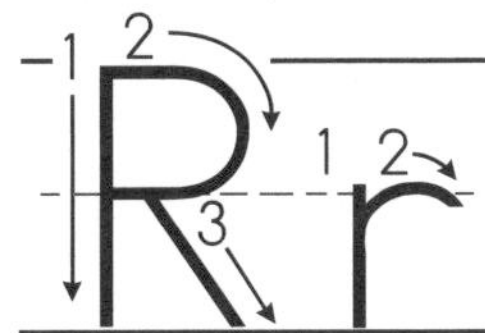

Rosie, the rabbit

I am Rosie, the rabbit.
Let's play a game.
Listen to the /r/ sound in my name.

Aa	Bb	Cc	Dd	Ee	Ff	Gg
Hh	Ii	Jj	Kk	Ll	Mm	Nn
Oo	Pp	Qq	Rr	Ss	Tt	Uu
Vv	Ww	Xx	Yy	Zz		

Rosie, the rabbit

rat

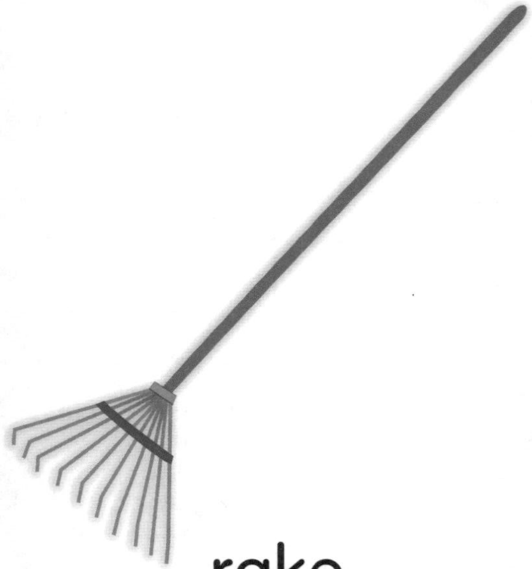

rake

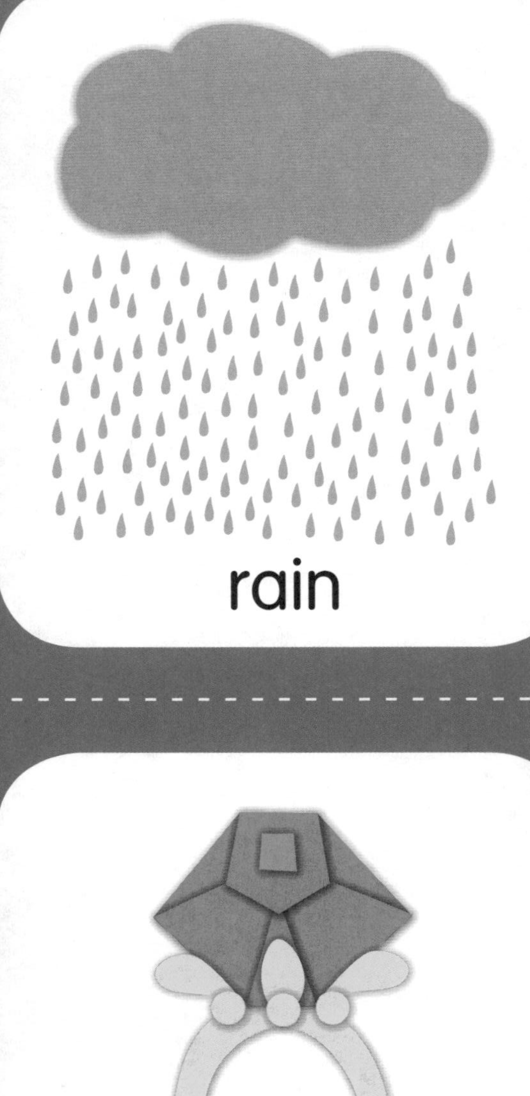

rain

rose

robot

ring

Rr

Look at Rosie, the rabbit.
Think of her name.
What other word
starts the same?

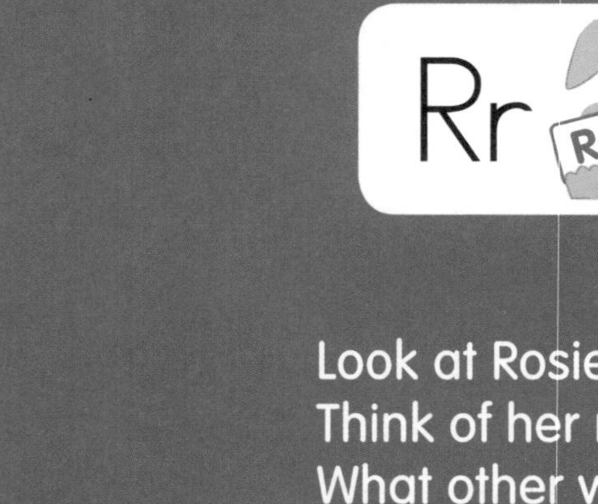
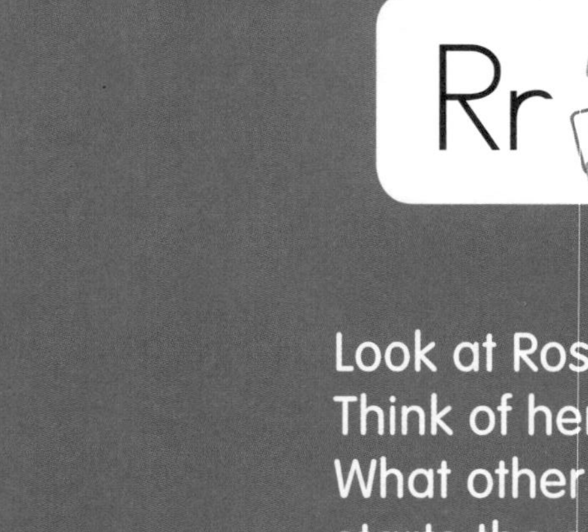

Rr

Look at Rosie, the rabbit.
Think of her name.
What other word
starts the same?

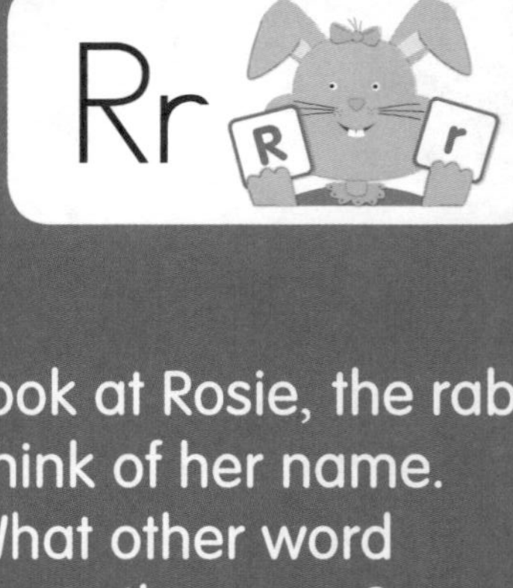

Rr

Look at Rosie, the rabbit.
Think of her name.
What other word
starts the same?

Rr

Look at Rosie, the rabbit.
Think of her name.
What other word
starts the same?

Rr

Look at Rosie, the rabbit.
Think of her name.
What other word
starts the same?

Rr

Look at Rosie, the rabbit.
Think of her name.
What other word
starts the same?

Ss Let's meet Skippy, the skunk

1. **See and Say Ss**
Introduce the puppet. Say, *Let's meet Skippy, the skunk.* Point to the letters on the puppet and say that every letter of the alphabet has two forms: big (capital) and little (lowercase). Recite the chant on the back of the puppet and help students practice the /s/ sound.

2. **How to Write Ss**
Trace the letters on the puppet with your finger to show the correct way to form capital **S** and lowercase **s**. Have students use their fingers in the air to form the letters with you. Verbalize the movements as you go. Say, for example, *Capital* ***S*** *begins near the top and curves up and around, and then down and around,* etc.

3. **Ss's Place in the Alphabet**
Use the back of the puppet to show **Ss**'s relative position in the alphabet. Have students sing the alphabet song and clap when they say **Ss**.

4. **Ss as an Initial Sound**
Point to the words on the puppet as you say, *The letter* ***Ss*** *makes the /s/ sound heard in* ***Skippy*** *and* ***skunk****.* Emphasize the beginning sound when you say the words. Then run your finger under the name **Skippy**, emphasizing the pronunciation of each letter. Now read the word **skunk** the same way. After reading each word, ask students, *Where do you hear the /s/ sound?*

Use the picture cards to identify other words that begin with the /s/ sound. Recite the chant on the back of each card as you show the card to the students. Say the word and have them echo you.

After you identify the initial /s/ sound for each card, place the card in the puppet's front pocket.

5. **Review**
Help students make their take-home mini-puppets. Then teach students the chant on the back of the mini-puppet and guide them through the activities to review the name, formation, and sound of **Ss**.

Trace and write the letters.

S s Ss

I am Skippy, the skunk.
Say my name.
What other words start the same?

Color the ones that begin with /s/.

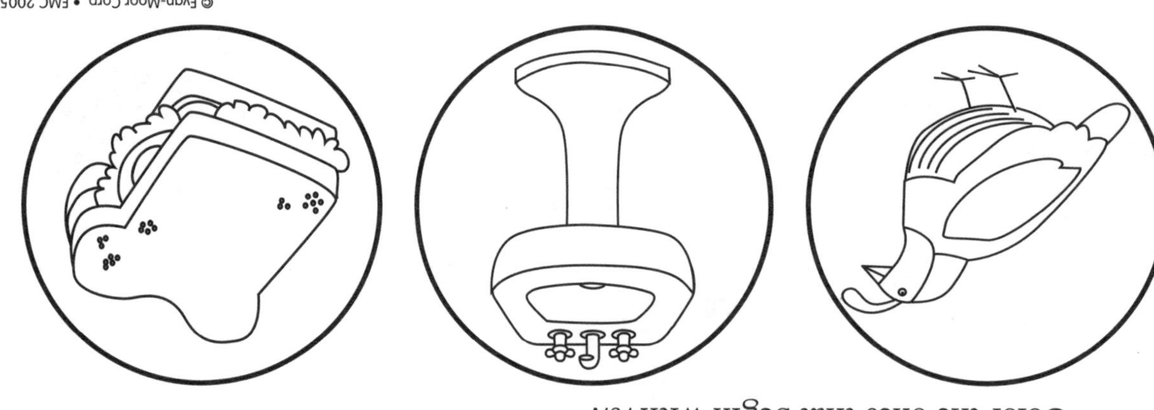

fold

I am Skippy.

I am a skunk.

Note: Cut along dashed lines. Glue figure to front of construction paper mitt, above the pocket. *(See page 7 for mitt template and instructions.)*

Note: Cut along dashed lines. Glue name strip across front pocket of construction paper mitt. Glue rhyme and alphabet chart to back of mitt, above the pocket. *(See page 7 for mitt template and instructions.)*

Ss

Skippy, the skunk

I am Skippy, the skunk.
Let's play a game.
Listen to the /s/ sound in my name.

Aa	Bb	Cc	Dd	Ee	Ff	Gg
Hh	Ii	Jj	Kk	Ll	Mm	Nn
Oo	Pp	Qq	Rr	Ss	Tt	Uu
Vv	Ww	Xx	Yy	Zz		

Skippy, the skunk

sink

scissors

sandwich

sun

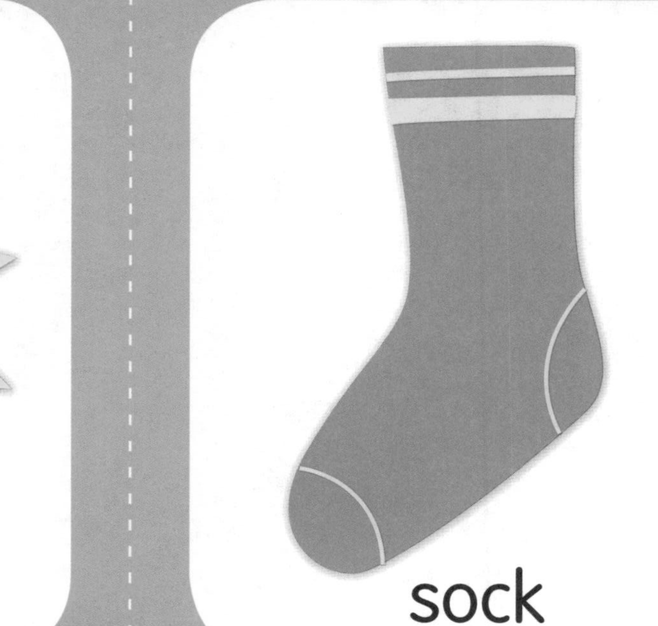

sock

six

Look at Skippy, the skunk.
Think of his name.
What other word
starts the same?

Look at Skippy, the skunk.
Think of his name.
What other word
starts the same?

Look at Skippy, the skunk.
Think of his name.
What other word
starts the same?

Look at Skippy, the skunk.
Think of his name.
What other word
starts the same?

Look at Skippy, the skunk.
Think of his name.
What other word
starts the same?

Look at Skippy, the skunk.
Think of his name.
What other word
starts the same?

Tt Let's meet Tootie, the turtle

1. **See and Say Tt**
   Introduce the puppet. Say, *Let's meet Tootie, the turtle.* Point to the letters on the puppet and say that every letter of the alphabet has two forms: big (capital) and little (lowercase). Recite the chant on the back of the puppet and help students practice the /t/ sound.

2. **How to Write Tt**
   Trace the letters on the puppet with your finger to show the correct way to form capital **T** and lowercase **t**. Have students use their fingers in the air to form the letters with you. Verbalize the movements as you go. Say, for example, *Capital **T** starts with a straight stick down, then add a cap across the top,* etc.

3. **Tt's Place in the Alphabet**
   Use the back of the puppet to show **Tt**'s relative position in the alphabet. Have students sing the alphabet song and clap when they say **Tt**.

4. **Tt as an Initial Sound**
   Point to the words on the puppet as you say, *The letter **Tt** makes the /t/ sound heard in **Tootie** and **turtle**.* Emphasize the beginning sound when you say the words. Then run your finger under the name **Tootie**, emphasizing the pronunciation of each letter. Now read the word **turtle** the same way. After reading each word, ask students, *Where do you hear the /t/ sound?*

   Use the picture cards to identify other words that begin with the /t/ sound. Recite the chant on the back of each card as you show the card to the students. Say the word and have them echo you.

   After you identify the initial /t/ sound for each card, place the card in the puppet's front pocket.

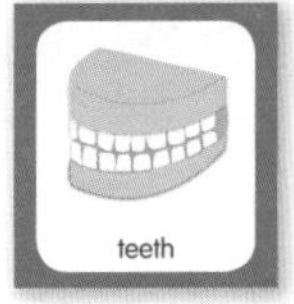

5. **Review**
   Help students make their take-home mini-puppets. Then teach students the chant on the back of the mini-puppet and guide them through the activities to review the name, formation, and sound of **Tt.**

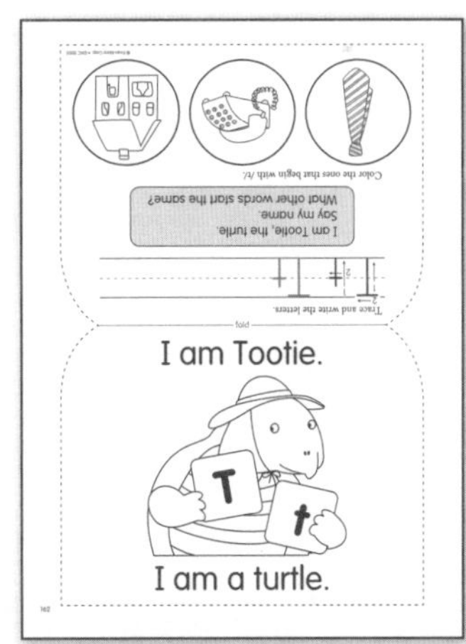

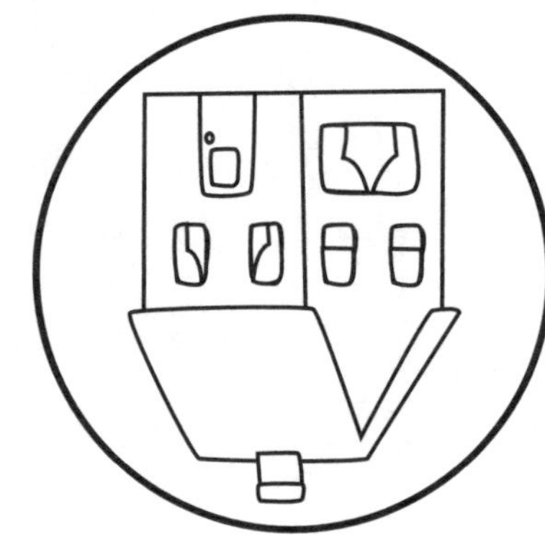

Color the ones that begin with /t/.

I am Tootie, the turtle.
Say my name.
What other words start the same?

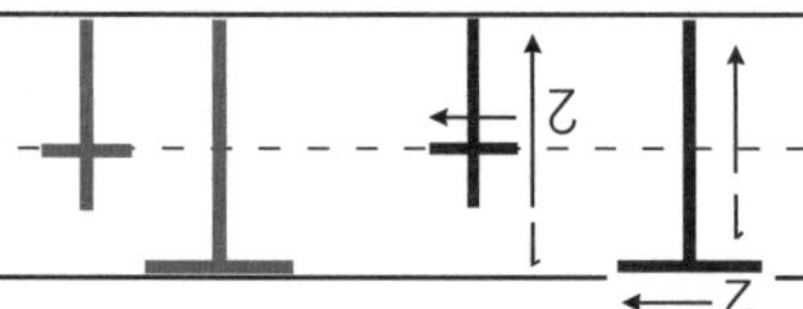

Trace and write the letters.

fold

I am Tootie.

I am a turtle.

Note: Cut along dashed lines. Glue figure to front of construction paper mitt, above the pocket.
(See page 7 for mitt template and instructions.)

Note: Cut along dashed lines. Glue name strip across front pocket of construction paper mitt. Glue rhyme and alphabet chart to back of mitt, above the pocket. *(See page 7 for mitt template and instructions.)*

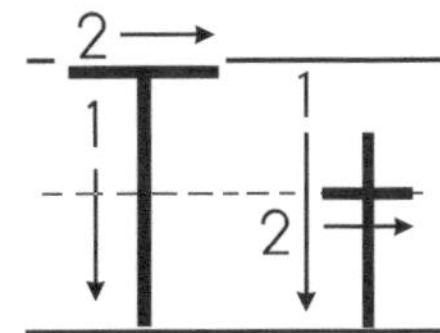

Tootie, the turtle

I am Tootie, the turtle.
Let's play a game.
Listen to the /t/ sound in my name.

Aa	Bb	Cc	Dd	Ee	Ff	Gg
Hh	Ii	Jj	Kk	Ll	Mm	Nn
Oo	Pp	Qq	Rr	Ss	Tt	Uu
Vv	Ww	Xx	Yy	Zz		

Tootie, the turtle

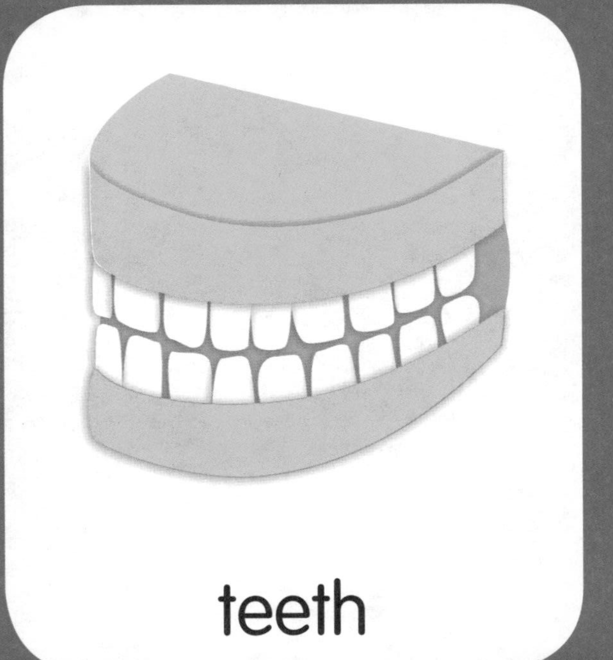

teeth

tail

table

tie

tent

telephone

Look at Tootie, the turtle.
Think of her name.
What other word
starts the same?

Look at Tootie, the turtle.
Think of her name.
What other word
starts the same?

© Evan-Moor Corp. • EMC 2005

Look at Tootie, the turtle.
Think of her name.
What other word
starts the same?

© Evan-Moor Corp. • EMC 2005

Look at Tootie, the turtle.
Think of her name.
What other word
starts the same?

© Evan-Moor Corp. • EMC 2005

Look at Tootie, the turtle.
Think of her name.
What other word
starts the same?

© Evan-Moor Corp. • EMC 2005

Look at Tootie, the turtle.
Think of her name.
What other word
starts the same?

© Evan-Moor Corp. • EMC 2005

Uu Let's meet Uncle Buck

1. **See and Say Uu**
   Introduce the puppet. Say, *Let's meet Uncle Buck.* Point to the letters on the puppet and say that every letter of the alphabet has two forms: big (capital) and little (lowercase). Recite the chant on the back of the puppet and help students practice the short **u** sound.

2. **How to Write Uu**
   Trace the letters on the puppet with your finger to show the correct way to form capital **U** and lowercase **u**. Have students use their fingers in the air to form the letters with you. Verbalize the movements as you go. Say, for example, *Capital* ***U*** *begins at the top, slides down, and then curves back up to the top*, etc.

short /u/ long /ū/

umbrella

3. **Uu's Place in the Alphabet**
   Use the back of the puppet to show **Uu**'s relative position in the alphabet. Have students sing the alphabet song and clap when they say **Uu**.

4. **Short Uu as an Initial Sound**
   Point to the name on the puppet as you say, *Sometimes, the letter* ***Uu*** *makes the /u/ sound heard in* ***Uncle****.* Emphasize the beginning sound when you say the word. Then run your finger under the word **Uncle**, emphasizing the pronunciation of each letter. Ask students, *Where do you hear the /u/ sound?* You could also ask students where they hear the /u/ sound in **Buck** (in the middle).

   Use the picture cards to identify other words that begin with the /u/ sound. Recite the chant on the back of each card as you show the card to the students. Say the word and have them echo you.

   Place the three cards that show /u/ (short **u**) words in the puppet's front pocket. Save the three cards with /ū/ (long **u**) words to introduce later. *(See page 218.)*

5. **Review**
   Help students make their take-home mini-puppets. Then teach students the chant on the back of the mini-puppet and guide them through the activities to review the name, formation, and sound of **Uu**.

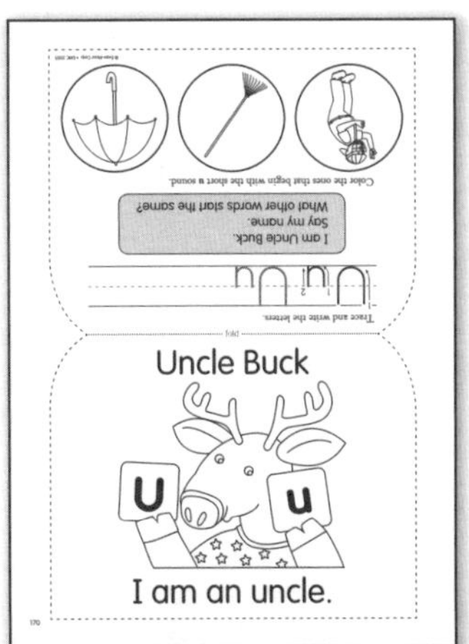

Trace and write the letters.

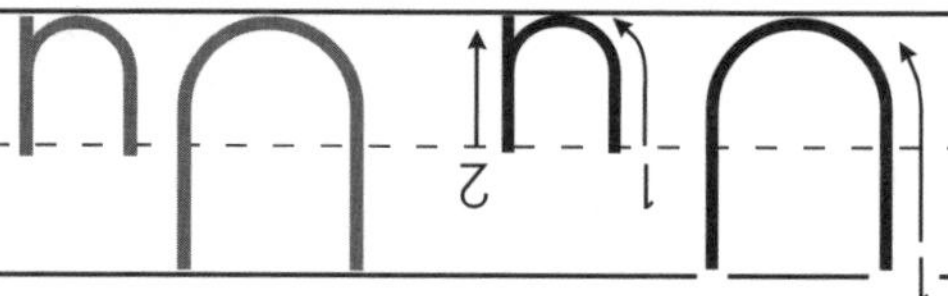

I am Uncle Buck.
Say my name.
What other words start the same?

Color the ones that begin with the short **u** sound.

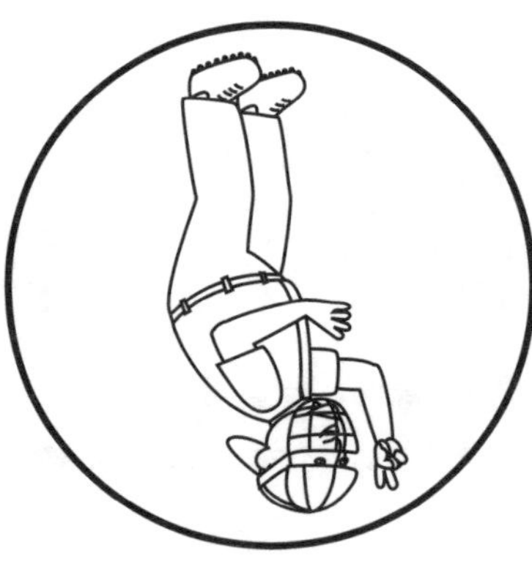

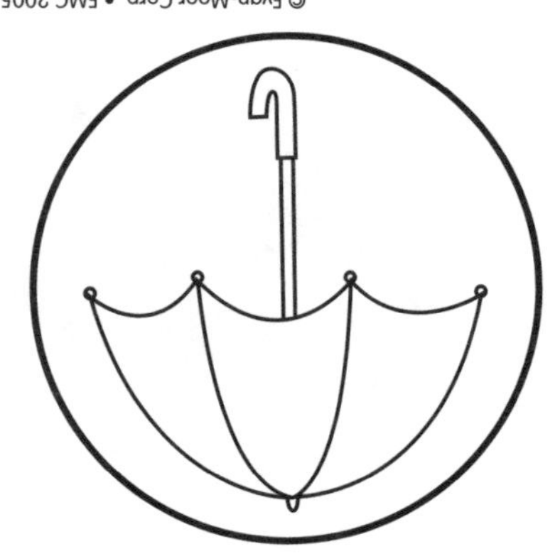

fold

Uncle Buck

I am an uncle.

Note: Cut along dashed lines. Glue figure to front of construction paper mitt, above the pocket. *(See page 7 for mitt template and instructions.)*

Note: Cut along dashed lines. Glue name strip across front pocket of construction paper mitt. Glue rhyme and alphabet chart to back of mitt, above the pocket. *(See page 7 for mitt template and instructions.)*

Uncle Buck

I am Uncle Buck.
Let's play a game.
Listen to the /u/ sound in my name.

Aa	Bb	Cc	Dd	Ee	Ff	Gg
Hh	Ii	Jj	Kk	Ll	Mm	Nn
Oo	Pp	Qq	Rr	Ss	Tt	Uu
Vv	Ww	Xx	Yy	Zz		

Uncle Buck

up

umpire

umbrella

United States

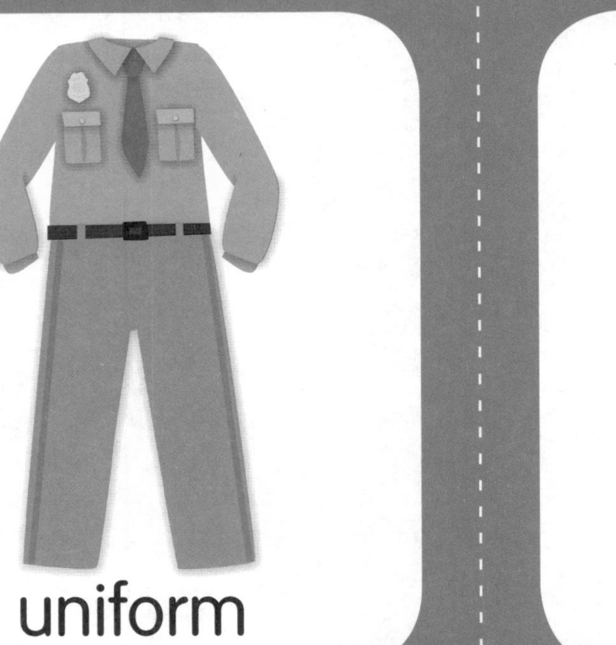

uniform

ukulele

Look at Uncle Buck.
Think of his name.
What other word
starts the same?

Look at Uncle Buck.
Think of his name.
What other word
starts the same?

© Evan-Moor Corp. • EMC 2005

Look at Uncle Buck.
Think of his name.
What other word
starts the same?

© Evan-Moor Corp. • EMC 2005

Look at Umi, the unicorn.
Think of her name.
What other word
starts the same?

© Evan-Moor Corp. • EMC 2005

Look at Umi, the unicorn.
Think of her name.
What other word
starts the same?

© Evan-Moor Corp. • EMC 2005

Look at Umi, the unicorn.
Think of her name.
What other word
starts the same?

© Evan-Moor Corp. • EMC 2005

Vv Let's meet Victor, the vulture

1. **See and Say Vv**
   Introduce the puppet. Say, *Let's meet Victor, the vulture.* Point to the letters on the puppet and say that every letter of the alphabet has two forms: big (capital) and little (lowercase). Recite the chant on the back of the puppet and help students practice the /v/ sound.

2. **How to Write Vv**
   Trace the letters on the puppet with your finger to show the correct way to form capital **V** and lowercase **v**. Have students use their fingers in the air to form the letters with you. Verbalize the movements as you go. Say, for example, *Capital V starts at the top, make a slanted line down, then go back to the top and make another slanted line to form a point,* etc.

3. **Vv's Place in the Alphabet**
   Use the back of the puppet to show **Vv**'s relative position in the alphabet. Have students sing the alphabet song and clap when they say **Vv**.

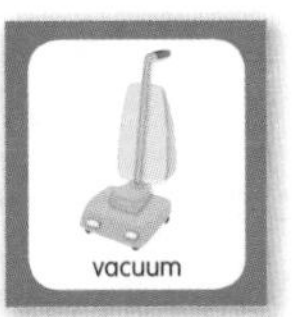

4. **Vv as an Initial Sound**
   Point to the words on the puppet as you say, *The letter **Vv** makes the /v/ sound heard in **Victor** and **vulture**.* Emphasize the beginning sound when you say the words. Then run your finger under the name **Victor**, emphasizing the pronunciation of each letter. Now read the word **vulture** the same way. After reading each word, ask students, *Where do you hear the /v/ sound?*

   Use the picture cards to identify other words that begin with the /v/ sound. Recite the chant on the back of each card as you show the card to the students. Say the word and have them echo you.

   After you identify the initial /v/ sound for each card, place the card in the puppet's front pocket.

5. **Review**
   Help students make their take-home mini-puppets. Then teach students the chant on the back of the mini-puppet and guide them through the activities to review the name, formation, and sound of **Vv**.

Trace and write the letters.

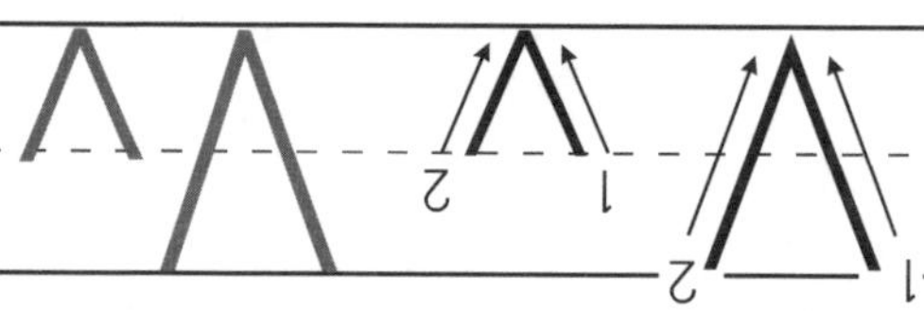

I am Victor, the vulture.
Say my name.
What other words start the same?

Color the ones that begin with /v/.

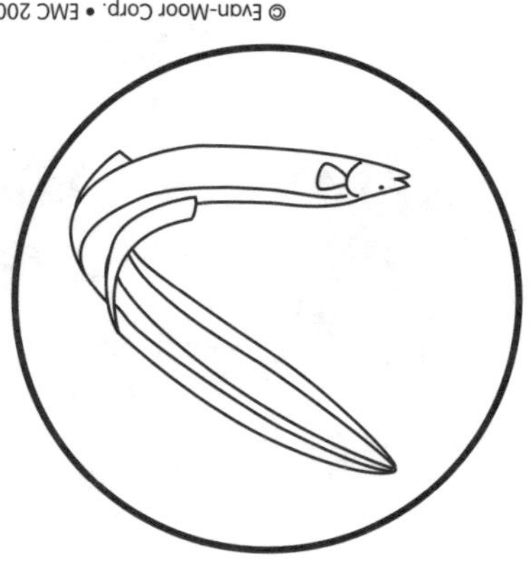

fold

I am Victor.

I am a vulture.

Note: Cut along dashed lines. Glue figure to front of construction paper mitt, above the pocket. *(See page 7 for mitt template and instructions.)*

Note: Cut along dashed lines. Glue name strip across front pocket of construction paper mitt. Glue rhyme and alphabet chart to back of mitt, above the pocket.
(See page 7 for mitt template and instructions.)

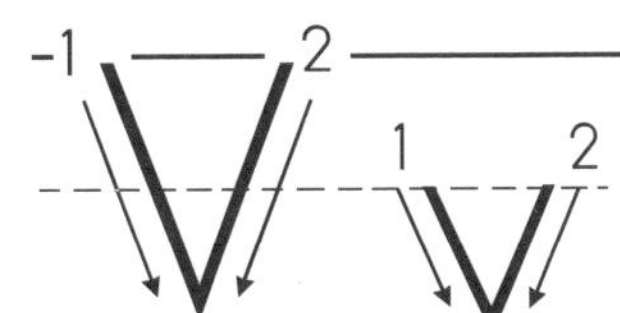

Victor, the vulture

I am Victor, the vulture.
Let's play a game.
Listen to the /v/ sound in my name.

Aa	Bb	Cc	Dd	Ee	Ff	Gg
Hh	Ii	Jj	Kk	Ll	Mm	Nn
Oo	Pp	Qq	Rr	Ss	Tt	Uu
Vv	Ww	Xx	Yy	Zz		

Victor, the vulture

vase

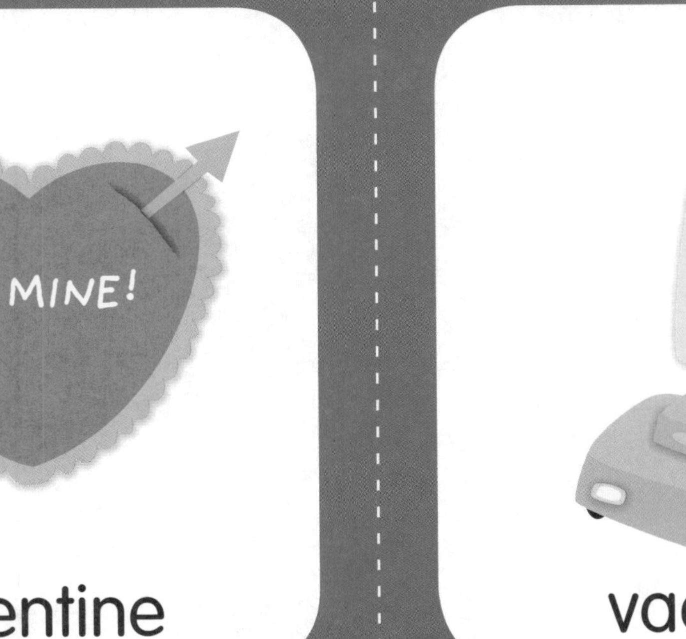

valentine

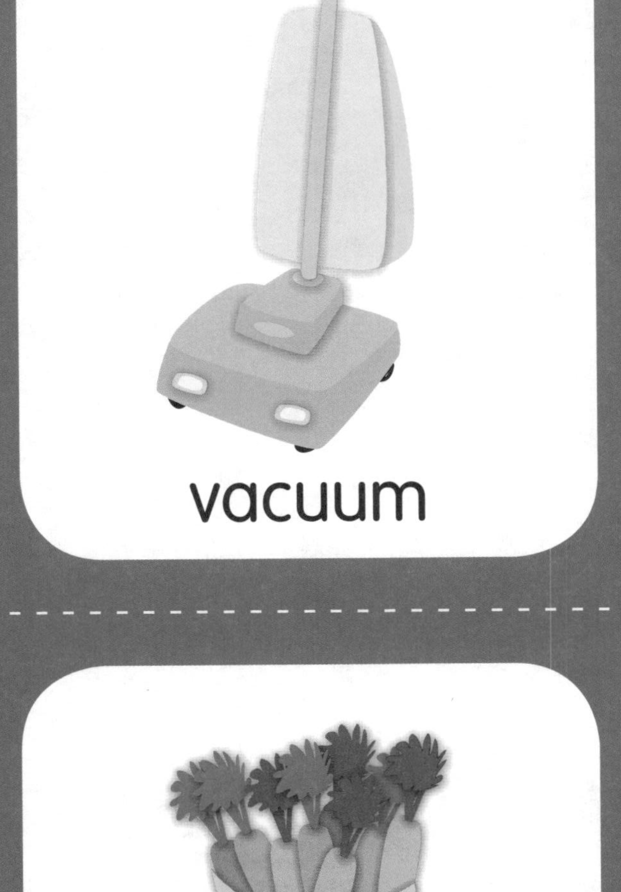

vacuum

volcano

violin

vegetables

Look at Victor, the vulture.
Think of his name.
What other word
starts the same?

Look at Victor, the vulture.
Think of his name.
What other word
starts the same?

© Evan-Moor Corp. • EMC 2005

Look at Victor, the vulture.
Think of his name.
What other word
starts the same?

© Evan-Moor Corp. • EMC 2005

Look at Victor, the vulture.
Think of his name.
What other word
starts the same?

© Evan-Moor Corp. • EMC 2005

Look at Victor, the vulture.
Think of his name.
What other word
starts the same?

© Evan-Moor Corp. • EMC 2005

Look at Victor, the vulture.
Think of his name.
What other word
starts the same?

© Evan-Moor Corp. • EMC 2005

Ww Let's meet Wanda, the walrus

1. See and Say Ww
Introduce the puppet. Say, *Let's meet Wanda, the walrus.* Point to the letters on the puppet and say that every letter of the alphabet has two forms: big (capital) and little (lowercase). Recite the chant on the back of the puppet and help students practice the /w/ sound.

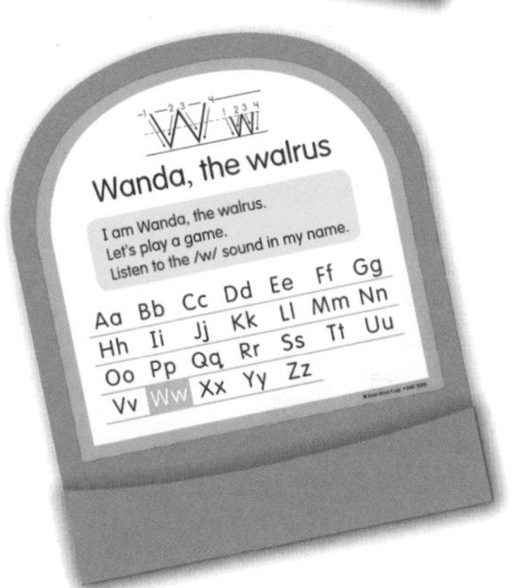

2. How to Write Ww
Trace the letters on the puppet with your finger to show the correct way to form capital **W** and lowercase **w**. Have students use their fingers in the air to form the letters with you. Verbalize the movements as you go. Say, for example, *Capital **W** starts at the top, make a slanted line down, then go back to the top three more times, making slanted lines that all touch each other,* etc.

3. Ww's Place in the Alphabet
Use the back of the puppet to show **Ww**'s relative position in the alphabet. Have students sing the alphabet song and clap when they say **Ww**.

4. Ww as an Initial Sound
Point to the words on the puppet as you say, *The letter **Ww** makes the /w/ sound heard in **Wanda** and **walrus**.* Emphasize the beginning sound when you say the words. Then run your finger under the name **Wanda**, emphasizing the pronunciation of each letter. Now read the word **walrus** the same way. After reading each word, ask students, *Where do you hear the /w/ sound?*

Use the picture cards to identify other words that begin with the /w/ sound. Recite the chant on the back of each card as you show the card to the students. Say the word and have them echo you.

After you identify the initial /w/ sound for each card, place the card in the puppet's front pocket.

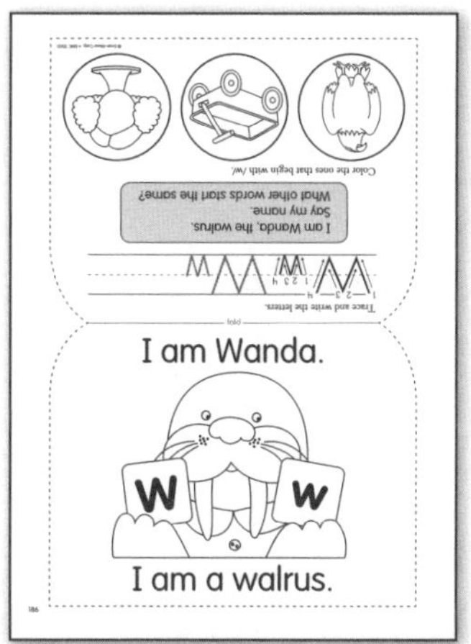

5. Review
Help students make their take-home mini-puppets. Then teach students the chant on the back of the mini-puppet and guide them through the activities to review the name, formation, and sound of **Ww**.

Trace and write the letters.

I am Wanda, the walrus.
Say my name.
What other words start the same?

Color the ones that begin with /w/.

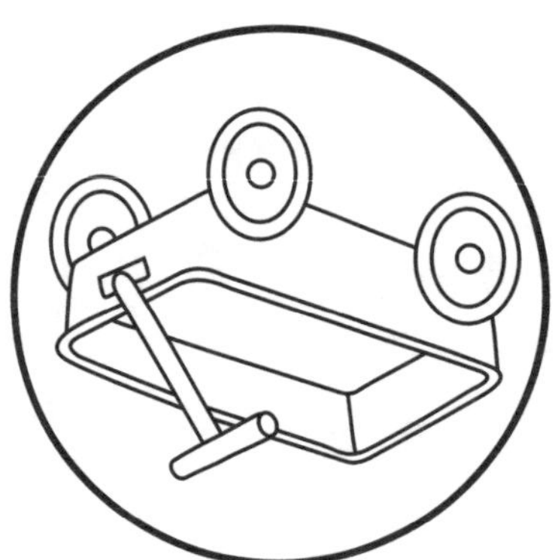

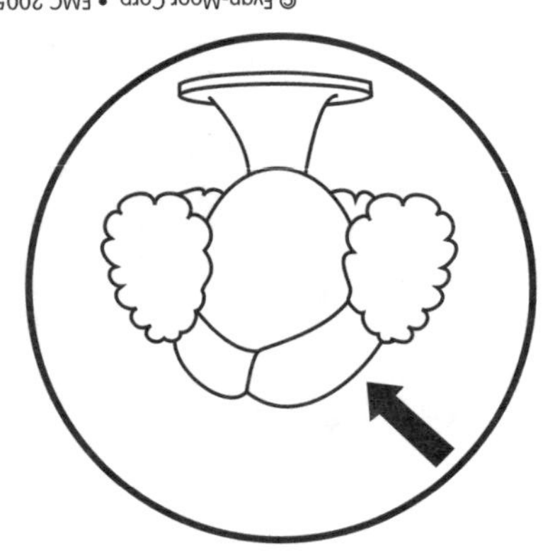

I am Wanda.

I am a walrus.

Note: Cut along dashed lines. Glue figure to front of construction paper mitt, above the pocket. *(See page 7 for mitt template and instructions.)*

Note: Cut along dashed lines. Glue name strip across front pocket of construction paper mitt. Glue rhyme and alphabet chart to back of mitt, above the pocket. *(See page 7 for mitt template and instructions.)*

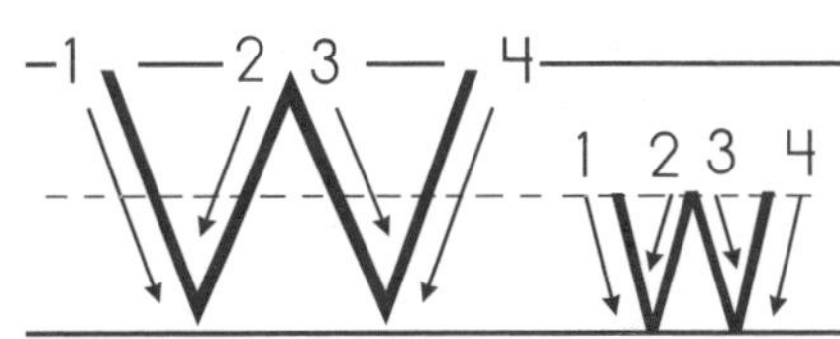

Wanda, the walrus

I am Wanda, the walrus.
Let's play a game.
Listen to the /w/ sound in my name.

Aa	Bb	Cc	Dd	Ee	Ff	Gg
Hh	Ii	Jj	Kk	Ll	Mm	Nn
Oo	Pp	Qq	Rr	Ss	Tt	Uu
Vv	Ww	Xx	Yy	Zz		

Wanda, the walrus

wash

wagon

wag

window

wig

web

Look at Wanda, the walrus.
Think of her name.
What other word
starts the same?

Look at Wanda, the walrus.
Think of her name.
What other word
starts the same?

Look at Wanda, the walrus.
Think of her name.
What other word
starts the same?

Look at Wanda, the walrus.
Think of her name.
What other word
starts the same?

Look at Wanda, the walrus.
Think of her name.
What other word
starts the same?

Look at Wanda, the walrus.
Think of her name.
What other word
starts the same?

1. **See and Say Xx**
   Introduce the puppet. Say, *Let's meet Roxie, the fox.* Point to the letters on the puppet and say that every letter of the alphabet has two forms: big (capital) and little (lowercase). Recite the chant on the back of the puppet and help students practice the /ks/ sound.

2. **How to Write Xx**
   Trace the letters on the puppet with your finger to show the correct way to form capital **X** and lowercase **x**. Have students use their fingers in the air to form the letters with you. Verbalize the movements as you go. Say, for example, *Capital **X** starts at the top, make a slanted line down, then back to the top and make a slanted line across,* etc.

3. **Xx's Place in the Alphabet**
   Use the back of the puppet to show **Xx**'s relative position in the alphabet. Have students sing the alphabet song and clap when they say **Xx**.

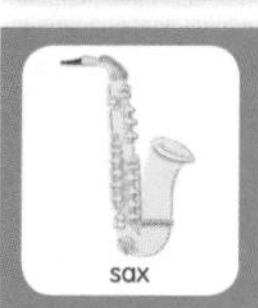

4. **Xx as an Ending Sound**
   Point to the word **fox** on the puppet as you say, *The letter **Xx** makes the /ks/ sound heard in **fox**.* Emphasize the ending sound when you say the word. Then run your finger under the word **fox**, emphasizing the pronunciation of each letter. Ask students, *Where do you hear the /ks/ sound?* You could also ask students where they hear the /ks/ sound in **Roxie** (in the middle).

   Use the picture cards to identify other words that end with the /ks/ sound. Recite the chant on the back of each card as you show the card to the students. Say the word and have them echo you.

   After you identify the ending /ks/ sound for each card, place the card in the puppet's front pocket.

5. **Review**
   Help students make their take-home mini-puppets. Then teach them the chant on the back of the mini-puppet and guide them through the activities to review the name, formation, and sound of **Xx**.

Trace and write the letters.

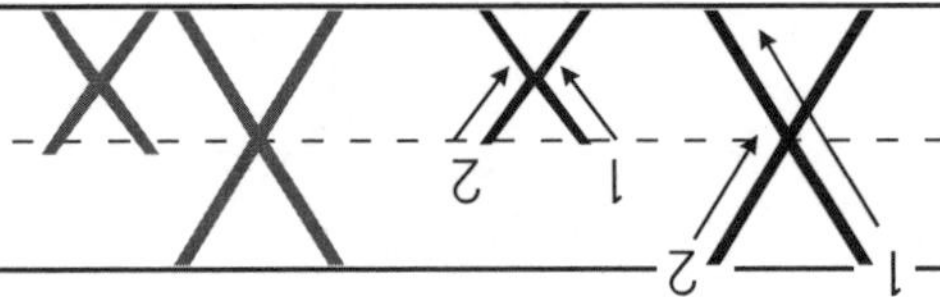

I am Roxie, the fox.
Say my name.
What other words end the same?

Color the ones that end with /ks/.

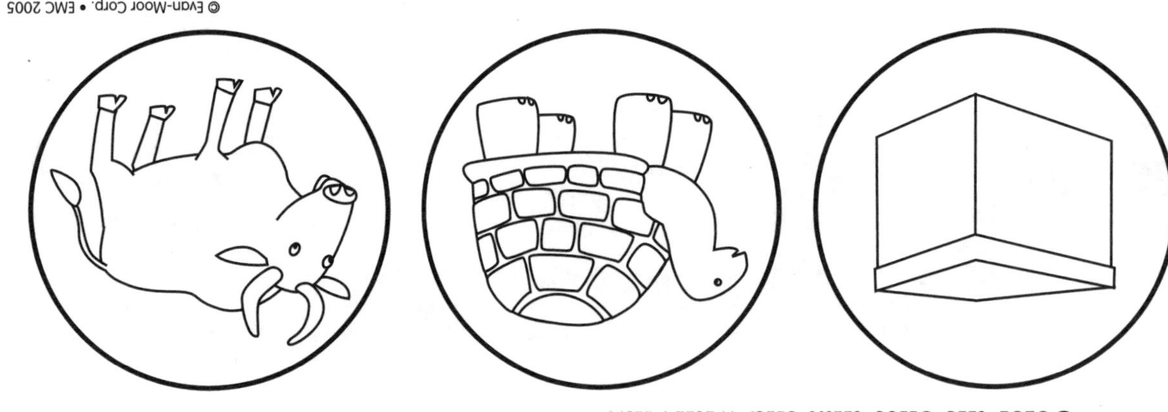

fold

I am Roxie.

I am a fox.

Note: Cut along dashed lines. Glue figure to front of construction paper mitt, above the pocket. *(See page 7 for mitt template and instructions.)*

Note: Cut along dashed lines. Glue name strip across front pocket of construction paper mitt. Glue rhyme and alphabet chart to back of mitt, above the pocket. *(See page 7 for mitt template and instructions.)*

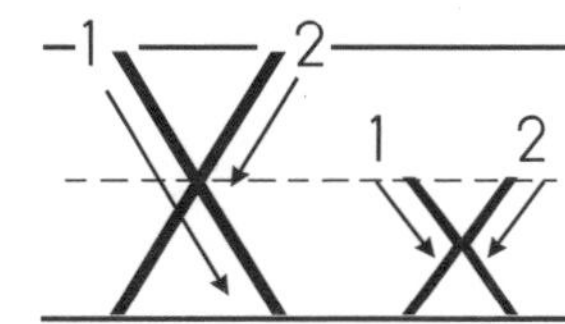

Roxie, the fox

I am Roxie, the fox.
Let's play a game.
Listen to the /ks/ sound in my name.

Aa	Bb	Cc	Dd	Ee	Ff	Gg
Hh	Ii	Jj	Kk	Ll	Mm	Nn
Oo	Pp	Qq	Rr	Ss	Tt	Uu
Vv	Ww	Xx	Yy	Zz		

Roxie, the fox

box

Max

ax

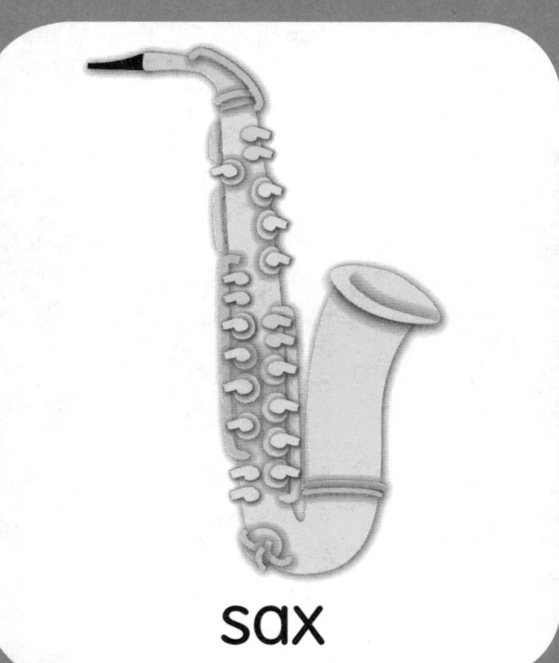
sax

ox

mix

Look at Roxie, the fox.
Think of her name.
What other word
ends the same?

Look at Roxie, the fox.
Think of her name.
What other word
ends the same?

© Evan-Moor Corp. • EMC 2005

Look at Roxie, the fox.
Think of her name.
What other word
ends the same?

© Evan-Moor Corp. • EMC 2005

Look at Roxie, the fox.
Think of her name.
What other word
ends the same?

© Evan-Moor Corp. • EMC 2005

Look at Roxie, the fox.
Think of her name.
What other word
ends the same?

© Evan-Moor Corp. • EMC 2005

Look at Roxie, the fox.
Think of her name.
What other word
ends the same?

© Evan-Moor Corp. • EMC 2005

Yy Let's meet Yogi, the yak

1. **See and Say Yy**
   Introduce the puppet. Say, *Let's meet Yogi, the yak.* Point to the letters on the puppet and say that every letter of the alphabet has two forms: big (capital) and little (lowercase). Recite the chant on the back of the puppet and help students practice the /y/ sound.

2. **How to Write Yy**
   Trace the letters on the puppet with your finger to show the correct way to form capital **Y** and lowercase **y**. Have students use their fingers in the air to form the letters with you. Verbalize the movements as you go. Say, for example, *Capital **Y** starts at the top, make two short slanted lines that meet in the middle, then add a short line down*, etc.

3. **Yy's Place in the Alphabet**
   Use the back of the puppet to show **Yy**'s relative position in the alphabet. Have students sing the alphabet song and clap when they say **Yy**.

yard

yo-yo

yarn

yogurt

yawn

yolk

4. **Yy as an Initial Sound**
   Point to the words on the puppet as you say, *The letter **Yy** makes the /y/ sound heard in **Yogi** and **yak**.* Emphasize the beginning sound when you say the words. Then run your finger under the name **Yogi**, emphasizing the pronunciation of each letter. Now read the word **yak** the same way. After reading each word, ask students, *Where do you hear the /y/ sound?*

   Use the picture cards to identify other words that begin with the /y/ sound. Recite the chant on the back of each card as you show the card to the students. Say the word and have them echo you.

   After you identify the initial /y/ sound for each card, place the card in the puppet's front pocket.

5. **Review**
   Help students make their take-home mini-puppets. Then teach students the chant on the back of the mini-puppet and guide them through the activities to review the name, formation, and sound of **Yy**.

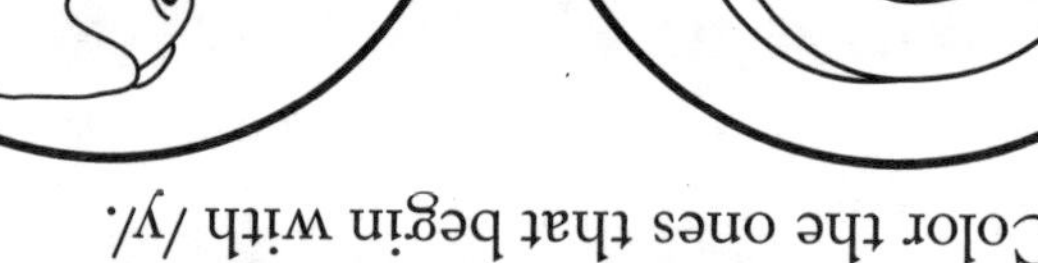

Color the ones that begin with /y/.

I am Yogi, the yak.
Say my name.
What other words start the same?

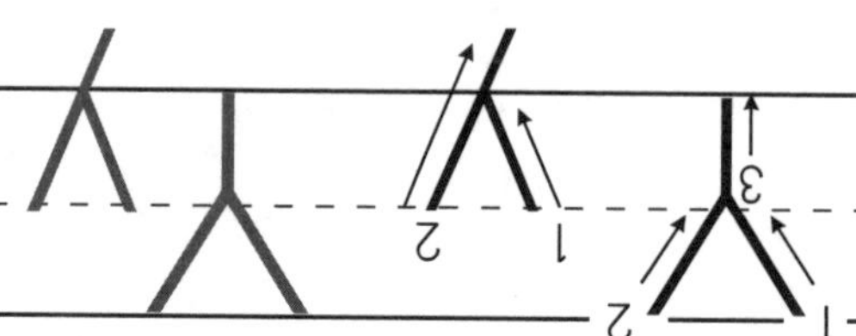

Trace and write the letters.

fold

I am Yogi.

I am a yak.

Note: Cut along dashed lines. Glue figure to front of construction paper mitt, above the pocket. *(See page 7 for mitt template and instructions.)*

Note: Cut along dashed lines. Glue name strip across front pocket of construction paper mitt. Glue rhyme and alphabet chart to back of mitt, above the pocket. *(See page 7 for mitt template and instructions.)*

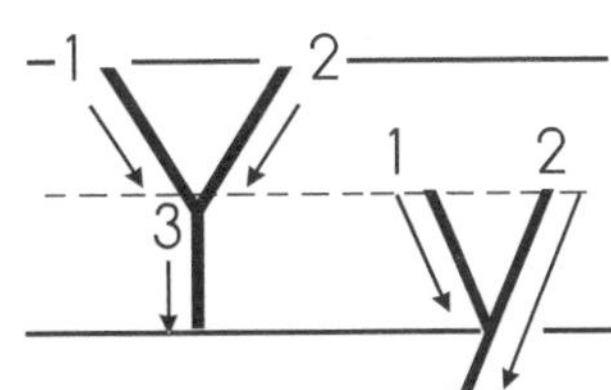

Yogi, the yak

I am Yogi, the yak.
Let's play a game.
Listen to the /y/ sound in my name.

Aa	Bb	Cc	Dd	Ee	Ff	Gg
Hh	Ii	Jj	Kk	Ll	Mm	Nn
Oo	Pp	Qq	Rr	Ss	Tt	Uu
Vv	Ww	Xx	Yy	Zz		

Yogi, the yak

yawn

yarn

yard

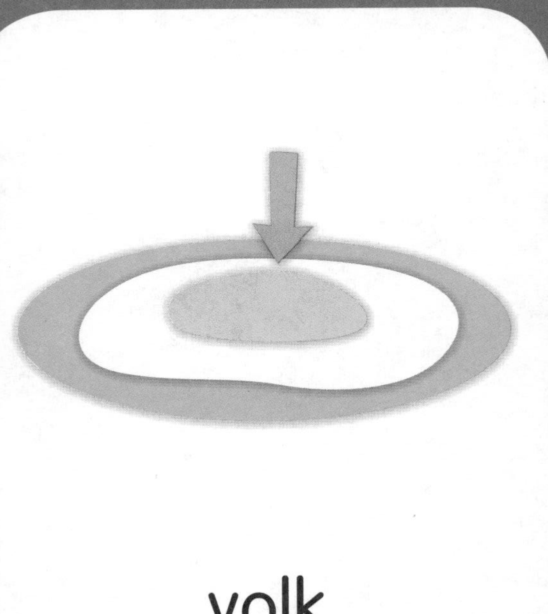
yolk

yogurt

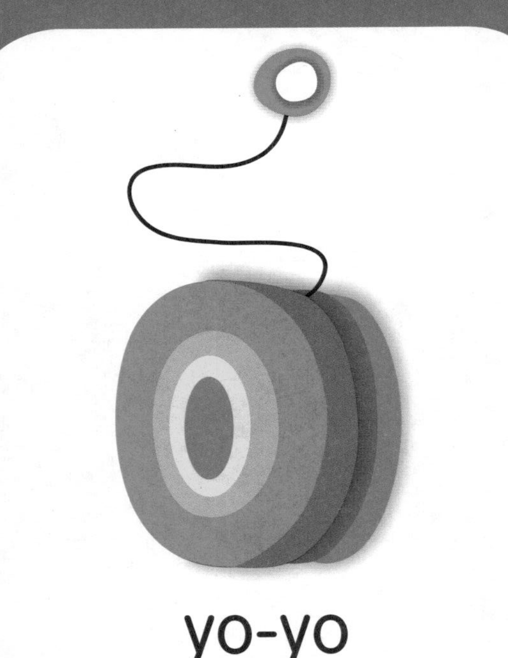
yo-yo

Look at Yogi, the yak.
Think of his name.
What other word
starts the same?

Look at Yogi, the yak.
Think of his name.
What other word
starts the same?

© Evan-Moor Corp. • EMC 2005

Look at Yogi, the yak.
Think of his name.
What other word
starts the same?

© Evan-Moor Corp. • EMC 2005

Look at Yogi, the yak.
Think of his name.
What other word
starts the same?

© Evan-Moor Corp. • EMC 2005

Look at Yogi, the yak.
Think of his name.
What other word
starts the same?

© Evan-Moor Corp. • EMC 2005

Look at Yogi, the yak.
Think of his name.
What other word
starts the same?

© Evan-Moor Corp. • EMC 2005

Zz Let's meet Zippy, the zebra

1. See and Say Zz

Introduce the puppet. Say, *Let's meet Zippy, the zebra.* Point to the letters on the puppet and say that every letter of the alphabet has two forms: big (capital) and little (lowercase). Recite the chant on the back of the puppet and help students practice the /z/ sound.

2. How to Write Zz

Trace the letters on the puppet with your finger to show the correct way to form capital **Z** and lowercase **z**. Have students use their fingers in the air to form the letters with you. Verbalize the movements as you go. Say, for example, *Capital* **Z** *begins with a line across the top, then make a slanted line down and a line across the bottom*, etc.

3. Zz's Place in the Alphabet

Use the back of the puppet to show **Zz**'s relative position in the alphabet. Have students sing the alphabet song and clap when they say **Zz**.

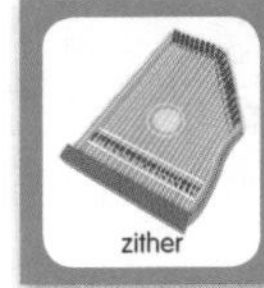

4. Zz as an Initial Sound

Point to the words on the puppet as you say, *The letter* **Zz** *makes the /z/ sound heard in* ***Zippy*** *and* ***zebra****.* Emphasize the beginning sound when you say each word. Then run your finger under the name **Zippy**, emphasizing the pronunciation of each letter. Now read the word **zebra** the same way. After reading each word, ask students, *Where do you hear the /z/ sound?*

Use the picture cards to identify other words that begin with the /z/ sound. Recite the chant on the back of each card as you show the card to the students. Say the word and have them echo you.

After you identify the initial /z/ sound for each card, place the card in the puppet's front pocket.

5. Review

Help students make their take-home mini-puppets. Then teach students the chant on the back of the mini-puppet and guide them through the activities to review the name, formation, and sound of **Zz**.

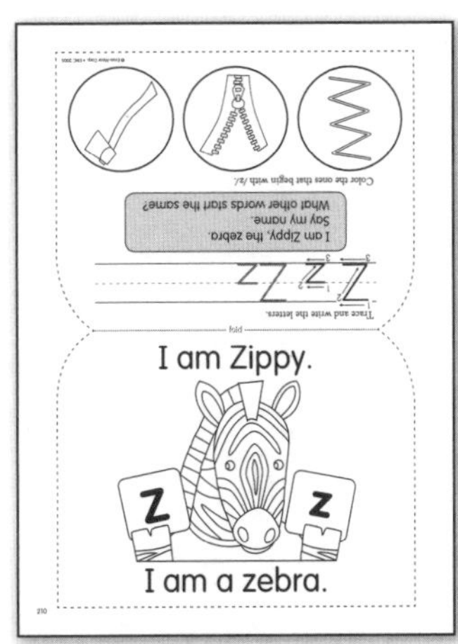

Trace and write the letters.

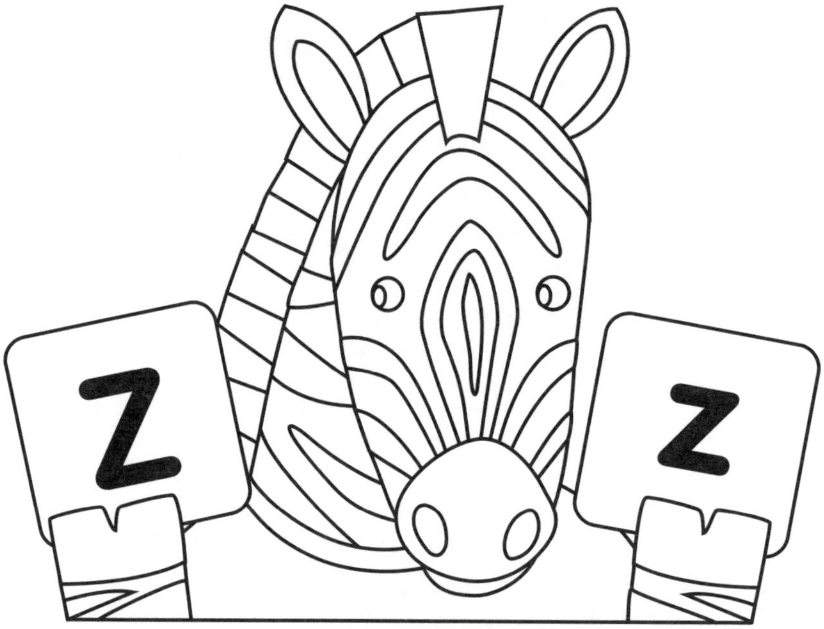

I am Zippy, the zebra.
Say my name.
What other words start the same?

Color the ones that begin with /z/.

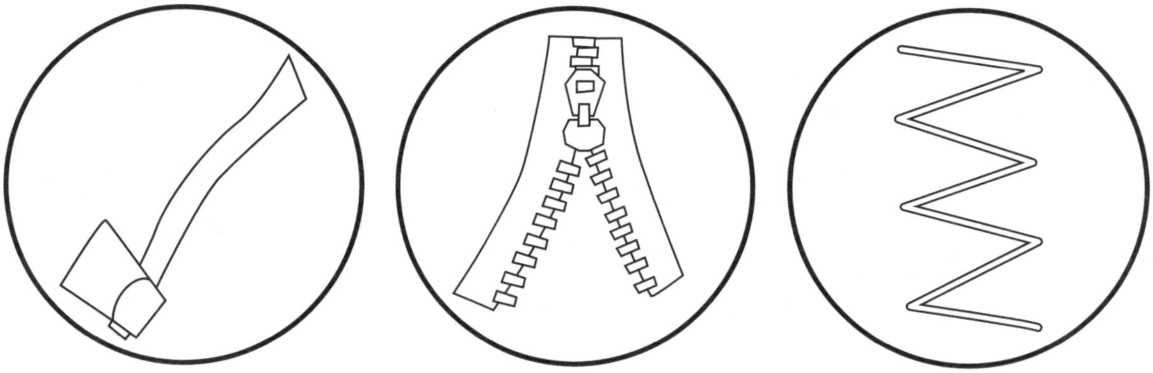

fold

I am Zippy.

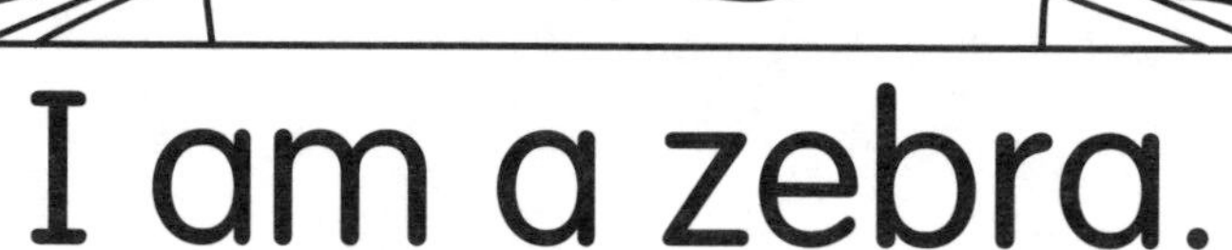

I am a zebra.

Note: Cut along dashed lines. Glue figure to front of construction paper mitt, above the pocket. *(See page 7 for mitt template and instructions.)*

Note: Cut along dashed lines. Glue name strip across front pocket of construction paper mitt. Glue rhyme and alphabet chart to back of mitt, above the pocket. *(See page 7 for mitt template and instructions.)*

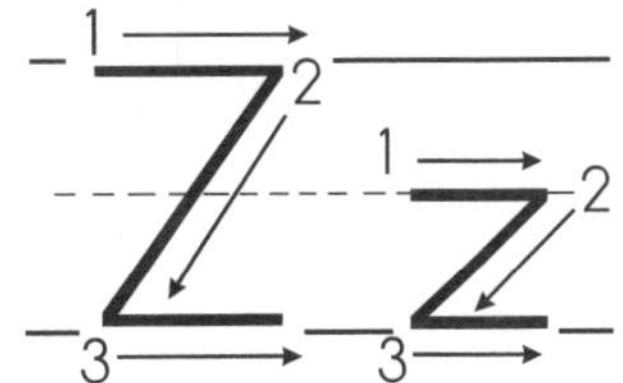

Zippy, the zebra

I am Zippy, the zebra.
Let's play a game.
Listen to the /z/ sound in my name.

Aa	Bb	Cc	Dd	Ee	Ff	Gg
Hh	Ii	Jj	Kk	Ll	Mm	Nn
Oo	Pp	Qq	Rr	Ss	Tt	Uu
Vv	Ww	Xx	Yy	Zz		

Zippy, the zebra

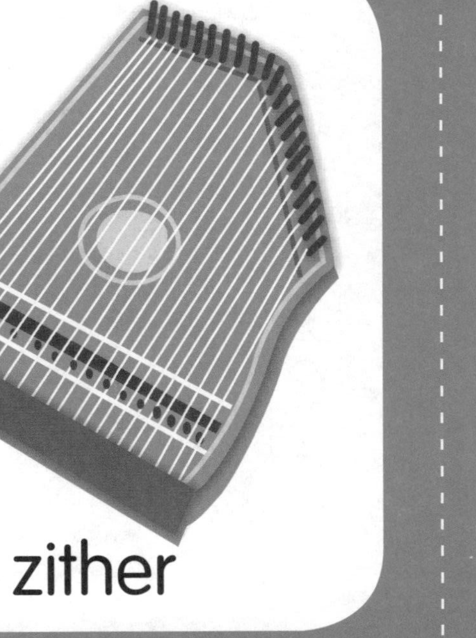

zither

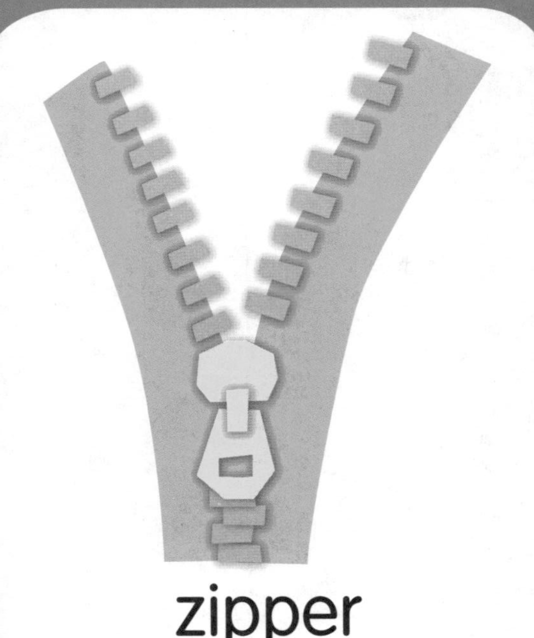
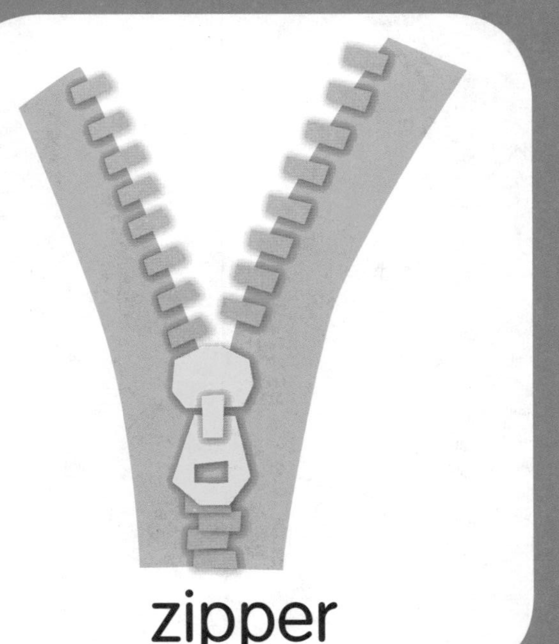

zipper

zero

zucchini

zoo

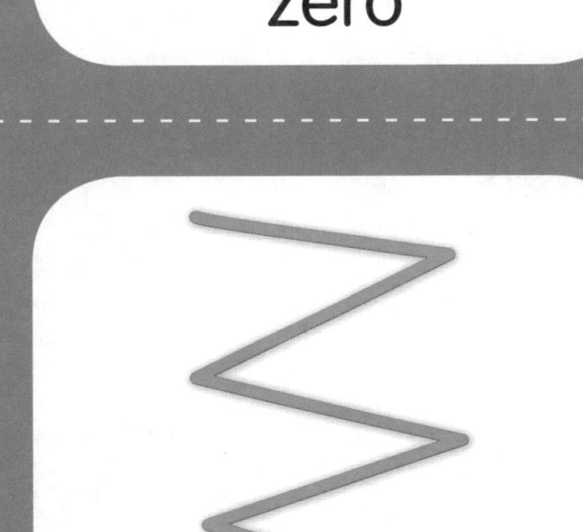

zigzag

Look at Zippy, the zebra.
Think of his name.
What other word
starts the same?

Look at Zippy, the zebra.
Think of his name.
What other word
starts the same?

Look at Zippy, the zebra.
Think of his name.
What other word
starts the same?

Look at Zippy, the zebra.
Think of his name.
What other word
starts the same?

Look at Zippy, the zebra.
Think of his name.
What other word
starts the same?

Look at Zippy, the zebra.
Think of his name.
What other word
starts the same?

How to Form the Letters

Long-Vowel Friends

The puppets for the letters **a**, **e**, **i**, **o**, and **u** provide activities that teach and reinforce short vowel sounds. Students must learn, however, that each vowel has both a short sound and a long sound.

After students master the short vowel sounds, use the Long-Vowel Friends cards on pages 219–224 to introduce the long vowel sounds. These full-color cards provide visual clues and help reinforce the sounds of long vowels. Each Long-Vowel Friend is designed to fit into the pocket of the matching short-vowel puppet.

The six picture cards provided for each vowel puppet include three initial short vowel words and three initial long vowel words. After the long vowels are introduced, students can use all six picture cards to compare vowel sounds.

	short vowels				long vowels		
/a/	apple	alligator	astronaut	/ā/	angel	acorn	apron
/e/	elbow	egg	end	/ē/	eagle	ear	eel
/i/	inch	ink	itch	/ī/	ice	iron	island
/o/	off on	ostrich	octopus	/ō/	oar	oboe	overalls
/u/	umbrella	umpire	up	/ū/	ukulele	uniform	United States

Eva
Long e sound

Amy
Long a sound

I am Amy, the ant.
Let's play a game.
Listen to the /ā/ sound
in my name.

picture cards

I am Eva, the elephant.
Let's play a game.
Listen to the /ē/ sound
in my name.

picture cards

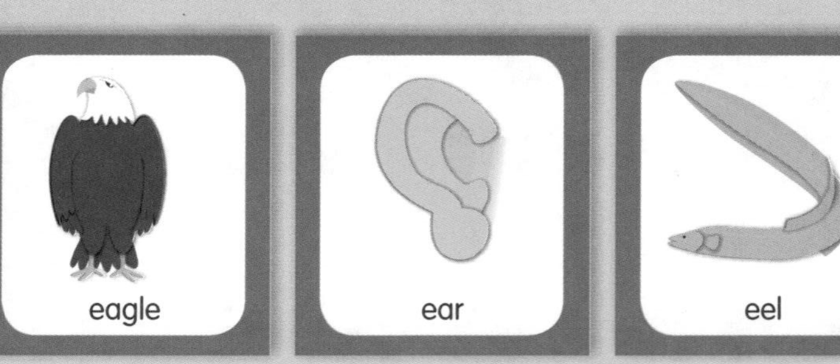

© Evan-Moor Corp. • EMC 2005

Oki
Long o sound

Ivy
Long i sound

I am Ivy, the iguana.
Let's play a game.
Listen to the /ī/ sound
in my name.

picture cards

I am Oki, the otter.
Let's play a game.
Listen to the /ō/ sound
in my name.

picture cards

oar

oboe

overalls

Umi
Long u sound

I am Umi, the unicorn.
Let's play a game.
Listen to the /ū/ sound
in my name.

picture cards